Praying the Rosary
for Inner Healing

Praying the Rosary
for Inner Healing

Fr. Dwight Longenecker

Our Sunday Visitor Publishing Division
Our Sunday Visitor, Inc.
Huntington, Indiana 46750

CONTENTS

PREFACE

The Christian faith is not just a theory or a good idea. It works. Through the life, death, and resurrection of Jesus Christ, God is transforming the world. He is doing this by transforming individuals into the likeness of Christ. The process of this transformation is a long, hard journey. It's the work of a lifetime. The first step of the journey is coming to realize that we need God's help. Then we have to accept what God has done for us in Christ. Next, with God's help, we embark on the adventure of faith. The end of our journey is what Jesus calls "abundant life" (see Jn 10:10). This is a life of total healing. It is a life of fullness. It means becoming all that God created us to be. This is not just a possibility, but a command. If you're a Christian, fullness of life and holiness is your calling.

We make the fastest progress on this journey on our knees. In other words, it is through prayer that we reach out for God, and he reaches down to heal us. The Rosary is one of the most effective and powerful ways to pray. As we pray the Rosary, God can heal us and transform our lives.

This little book shows you how to use the Rosary for healing. It comes from my own experience in prayer. Do not just read this book: use it to pray. And as you pray, may God touch and heal you and continue the work of transforming you into the likeness of his Son.

FR. DWIGHT LONGENECKER
Greenville, South Carolina
April 2007

INTRODUCTION

Jesus the Healer

Jesus Christ came to heal. He announced it himself when he stood up to read the lesson as he began his ministry in the synagogue in his hometown. He went to Nazareth, where he had been brought up, and on the Sabbath day he went into the synagogue, as was his custom. And he stood up to read. The scroll of the prophet Isaiah was handed to him. Unrolling it, he found the place where it was written:

"The Spirit of the Lord is upon me,
because he has anointed me to preach good news to the
poor.
He has sent me to proclaim release to the captives
and recovering of sight to the blind,
to set at liberty those who are oppressed,
to proclaim the acceptable year of the Lord." (Lk 4:18-19)

Jesus proved it throughout his ministry. Wherever he went, he healed people and set them free.

Jesus wasn't the only healer the world has seen. There have always been wonderworkers. There have always been men and women who have a natural gift to understand people and help them get better. There have always been doctors and wise people who have exercised healing gifts. There have also been shamans and showmen who would "heal" people through the power of suggestion and hypnosis. Others have healed through the power of demons, and their healing has always come at a price.

Jesus' healing power is different from all of these. The healing power of Jesus is unique. Jesus is the only one who heals by going to the root of illness and disease. Jesus understands that the root cause of all disease and distress is sin. As soon as we hear the word "sin," the red flag of guilt flies, and we get defensive. We don't need to be ashamed of the word "sin." Sin is simply the word we use for what has gone wrong with humanity. Sin is the twist in our god-like nature. It's the glitch in the system. It's the blemish on the faces of the beautiful sons and daughters of God that we were all created to be.

There's no point trying to deny the fact of sin. Sin is as ancient as the Garden of Eden and as fresh as today's headlines. Sin is a fact of life. It's the one Christian belief that no one can deny, because we all experience it firsthand every day.

Sin's Curse

Sin includes all of the things we do that we are ashamed of — but sin is bigger and simpler than that. The Bible puts it simply when it says that "all have sinned and fall short of the glory of God" (Rom 3:23). This is the basic definition of sin: we were created to share in the fullness of God's power, beauty, and glory, but we don't. We miss the mark. We are not all we can be — and left on our own, our condition gets worse, not better.

Missing the fullness of God's glory is bad enough, but the side effect of sin is that it causes pain and suffering. When there is something missing, we feel hunger, longing, and grief. When our lives go haywire because of sin, pain is the result; and when things continue to go wrong with no remedy, an inner illness develops. Eventually, we become numb to sin — and as we become numb to sin, we also become numb to the goodness of life. The joyful, hopeful, and youthful part of us starts to die. We become confused, the emptiness of our lives leads to despair, and eventually this inner illness causes spiritual death. That's why the Bible puts it quite simply when it says that "the wages of sin is death" (Rom 6:23).

It's easy to blame ourselves for the sin that causes illness, disease, and death, but it's a bit more complicated than that. We suffer from the wrong things we do, but we're caught up in more than just the individual sins we ourselves commit. We live with other people who are also sinful, and we live in a world that is shot through with evil — like a nasty virus. All of us are caught in a sticky spider's web of sin — and the more we struggle, the more entangled we become.

All of us suffer from four categories of sin.

The simplest sins are *the things we do wrong*. All of us miss the mark. We do things that seem pleasurable or good, but these actions injure ourselves or others in some way — even if we can't see it.

The second type of sin is *the good things we have left undone*. We all have fantastic potential that we have failed to realize. We're naturally lazy and we avoid the effort of doing positive good, and this absence of good is a very insidious kind of evil.

Many people are totally unaware of the third type of sin. This is *the bad things that are done to us*. Other people do us harm — sometimes intentionally, but very often unintentionally. These sins wound us deeply and cause our inner sin-illness to get worse.

Finally, we all suffer what might be called "general sin." We get infected, harmed, depressed, and weighed down by the everyday sin that is all around us and shot through this wicked world.

Worst of all, there is nothing we can do about this curse on our own. We can try very hard to be good, but that doesn't put right the inner wound. In the face of the sin problem, being good is like putting a Band-Aid on your belly to cure cancer. The illness of sin is deep and terminal, and it needs a cure far deeper and more costly than we can provide ourselves.

God's Cure

God saw mankind's sinful condition and provided the cure. Two thousand years ago, a baby girl was conceived by the union of a devout Jewish couple named Joachim and Anne. As the little girl was conceived, God touched her life and preserved her from the stain of original sin. The little girl was named Mary. By a miracle, Mary was brought into the world in the same pure condition as the first woman, Eve. Mary didn't suffer from sin's curse. This privilege was won for her by the terrible death her Son would eventually go through.

One of the effects of our sinful condition is that we are naturally biased toward the wrong choice. We are drawn toward sin more strongly than we are drawn toward the good. Because Mary was unsoiled by original sin, she did not have this inclination toward evil. She was able to see clearly and choose freely. She was able to say "yes" or "no" to God with a totally free choice. When the angel Gabriel brought God's message to her, she said "yes" to God, and God's Son was conceived in her womb. This miraculous conception was God's way of coming into the world to deal with the curse of sin once and for all.

The whole point of Jesus coming into the world was to solve the sin problem. Jesus was the antidote to sin's poison. He was the cure to sin's sickness and the warrior who defeated the dark Lord of hell. It was natural, therefore, for him to confront the symptoms of sin in his ministry. That's why he healed people, and that's why his healing was different from any others the world had ever seen — because he not only healed their physical illnesses, but in every case the healing was also linked with the forgiveness of sins.

When Mary's Son died on the cross, he took on the final battle with humanity's sin. Sin rose up and killed the one who was sinless. In this sacrifice, Jesus Christ took on himself the cancer of sin, and he suffered its result. But the Evil One overestimated himself. He forgot that evil cannot extinguish the good. What is essentially empty, negative, and false cannot overcome all that is abundant, positive, and true. The darkness cannot put out the light. It is simply impossible for evil to defeat goodness. That's why Jesus rose from the dead: because you cannot kill the one who is Life itself.

Life Heals

Jesus' victory over death planted a seed of new life in the hard soil of this broken world. From that point his healing was available for the whole of creation. The love and power of Christ healed people, and Jesus wants to heal us today.

His love can penetrate our lives and touch the wounds in our lives that are in areas so deep we don't even know about them. Do you remember the woman who crept up in the crowd to touch the hem of Jesus' cloak? She was forgiven and healed of a deep inner illness (see Mt 9:20-22). This is what Jesus can do for us. We can approach and touch the hem of Jesus' cloak too. Just as he turned and looked on her with compassion and knew all her problems in an instant, so he can turn and look on us with that same compassion and healing love.

How do we get in touch with the healing love of Christ? It's not easy. The way to Christ is full of obstacles. We can't see him clearly because of our misunderstandings. Sin blocks the way. We want his love and healing, but we are also afraid of what this might entail. We want him to heal us, but we're not sure we are ready for the total transformation that his healing will bring us. We're afraid of the total commitment he demands. Other duties crowd our lives; other interests distract us from his love. We're full of doubt, fear, anxiety — and we lack the faith and trust required to really reach out and touch him.

We can approach Jesus' healing power in various ways. First, we need to approach Jesus through the sacraments of the

Church. If we want his healing, we first need to receive him regularly through Communion. If we want this to be a complete meeting with Christ, we also have to meet him in the Sacrament of Reconciliation. There Jesus meets us and deals with the sin that blocks us from the fullness of his healing love.

Jesus also wants to meet us in the more intimate and personal aspects of our lives. He invites us to walk with him, and to meet him face-to-face. The best way to do this is by meditating on his life. When I say "meditate," I don't mean the type of meditation practiced by Eastern religions. That type of meditation involves emptying your mind. Christian meditation is different. Instead of emptying our mind, we fill it with the life of Christ. We do this by meditating on the gospel, and the best way to do this is through the Rosary.

A Mother's Prayer

A mother's prayer is an especially intimate one. From the fullness of her love for her children she is able to pray precisely for their needs. A mother's love for her children is simple, deep, and unconditional. She loves her children simply because they are her children. She can't help it. Loving and knowing them so deeply is all part of being a mother. Because of this, a mother's prayer is especially intimate, simple, deep, and unconditional. A mother prays simply by lifting the child up to God as a daily offering. "Here he is, dear God," the mother prays. "Do with him what you will. Heal him, love him, use him, and bring him to the fullness of your glory."

The Rosary is a simple way to put ourselves into the life of Christ, with Mary his mother. With the Rosary, we go through every stage of Jesus' life. With Mary, we go with him and make contact with his saving love. The gospels say that Mary saw all that was happening in her life and in her Son's life, and that she *pondered these things in her heart* (see Lk 2:51). As we pray the

Rosary, we "ponder these things" in our heart with Mary. As we do so, we go with her to meet Jesus, and through her prayers for us we experience his healing love in a powerful way.

Finally, our meditations bring us to the foot of the cross with Mary. From the cross, Jesus says to us: "Here is your mother" (see Jn 19:27). Because Mary is the perfect woman, she must also be the perfect mother. If she is the perfect mother, then her mother's prayer must also be the fullest and most whole and wonderful there is.

Mary is like the mother who goes with her injured child as they enter the hospital to be healed. Mary is like the loving sister or aunt who sits by the bedside as we endure a long illness. She is like one of Mother Teresa's Missionaries of Charity who care for the dying until the surgeon can come. She doesn't heal us. Jesus does. She is there as the vitally important sister, mother, nun, nurse, and friend. Her prayers are those of a mother for her children.

How I Met Mary

I first discovered the healing power of the Rosary when I was an Anglican minister. As a young man, sin played havoc with my life. I went through some dark times and spent time in counseling. My counselor was a wise old priest who advised me to start praying the Rosary. I discovered that the Joyful Mysteries of the Rosary took me into the first stages of Jesus' life and childhood. As I prayed through those stages, something mysterious happened. God's love began to seep into the early stages of my own life, and I began to experience healing from the deep hurts I had received in the very earliest foundation experiences of my life.

What I went through wasn't easy. God had to take me apart and put me back together again. Jesus was doing some serious spiritual surgery, and I was in spiritual intensive care. In the midst of it, I felt an abiding presence of love and concern by my side. I felt this as a feminine presence. Because I was from a Protestant background, I didn't know who or what this was. It was only later when I told my priest counselor that he smiled and said, "Our Lady's prayers for you have been so powerful!"

"Of course!" I thought. "The presence through all this was that of a mother. That's what it felt like!" Suddenly the floodgates opened, and the emotions I had been holding back gushed out in a fountain of healing. Only then did I begin to realize and accept the ministry of Jesus' mother in my life, and since then my devotion and love for her activity in the divine plan has grown through every aspect of my life of faith.

The Rosary has become an important part of my prayer life because it works. Mary said, "My soul magnifies the Lord" (Lk 1:46), and that is exactly what she does through the Rosary. She used the word "magnify" to mean "praise" or "exalt," but she "magnifies" the Lord in another way too. "Magnify" means "to make larger," and that's what Mary does in our lives: she makes Jesus larger and more real to us than we could ever imagine.

Every Step Along the Way

Through the Rosary, we go through every stage of Jesus' earthly life. Through the power of meditation, the Holy Spirit actually uses our minds to take us into the saving events of Jesus' life. Because he was sinless, Jesus' life was all that a human life should be. It was full, complete, and whole. It was mature, healthy, fulfilled, and balanced. Because he was God in human form, Jesus was radiantly alive, totally free — and abundantly, overwhelmingly human.

Because of this, when we enter into the stages of his life through the Rosary, we experience a life that is totally and abundantly whole. We experience life in its fullness, and we participate in the health, wholeness, and goodness of being fully alive and free. By entering into the wholeness of each stage of Jesus' life, we begin to share in his wholeness and health. As this happens, we are healed and made whole at a very deep level of our being. Pope John Paul the Great said about the Rosary: "The Rosary does indeed 'mark the rhythm of human life,' bringing it into harmony with the 'rhythm' of God's own life" (*Rosarium Virginis Mariae*, n. 25).

Long before I had read Pope John Paul's words, I had discovered this simple principle through my own experience of the Healing Rosary. I discovered the truth that as the meditations take us through every stage of Jesus' life, so they take us through every stage of our own lives. As we remember, with Jesus and Mary, the stages of our own life, all that was broken, faulty, or wounded at those stages of our lives can be healed.

By praying the Rosary in this way, we can gently pry open the dark cupboards of our hurt memories, fears, and sins. Once the injuries, sins, and painful memories from each stage are accessed, Christ's healing can begin. As Pope John Paul teaches, "It becomes natural [through the Rosary] to bring ... all the problems, anxieties, labors and endeavors which go to make up our lives. . . . To pray the Rosary is to hand over our burdens to the merciful hearts of Christ and his Mother" (*Rosarium Virginis Mariae*, n. 25).

As we do this, we are praying not only for ourselves, but for our families, our nation, and our world. If each of us, as individuals, goes through progressive stages of growth, so do groups of people. Pope John Paul the Great said, "At the same time our heart can embrace in the decades of the Rosary all the events that make up the lives of individuals, families, nations, the Church, and all mankind" (*Rosarium Virginis Mariae*, n. 2). Many popes and countless Christians have testified to the healing power of the Rosary. Why not join with them and begin to use the Rosary again in a new way?

A Word of Warning

I should give you a word of warning at this stage. From the very start, this book will take you to the depths. Jesus calls us to *cast out into the deep* (see Lk 5:4). However, if you are in a fragile or especially vulnerable emotional condition, tread carefully. Pray first for guidance, and embark on this healing journey only if you feel courageous enough to confront some aspects of life that may be disturbing. If you are in a vulnerable or fragile state, it is good to have the support of a wise and spiritual friend with whom to discuss what you discover. However, do not allow my word of warning to become an excuse for remaining where you are! God wants to heal you, but the time must be his time — and you must know when that is.

When you are ready, this book will help you to pray the Rosary for your own healing and for the healing of your family, your community, and your world. This is a practical book. It is not just theory. It works. Don't just read this book and put it away. Use it, tell others about it, and spread the word. If you have the courage to approach him and reach out to touch the hem of his cloak, Jesus really will turn, touch your life, forgive you, and heal you. The healing may take time. It may be painful — and the road to recovery may be long and hard — but Mary will be there at every step to help you discover a new life in Christ that will be radiant, abundant, and free.

How to Use this Book

- The first section of the book reminds you how to pray the Rosary. Even if you know how to pray the Rosary, skim through this section because it includes some special pointers for using the Rosary for healing.

- The main part of the book takes you through all twenty mysteries of the Rosary.
- The title of each mystery is matched with a stage of our lives.
- The section on each mystery begins with a Scripture reference that reminds us of that stage.
- On the opposite page there is an illustration of the event to help you visualize your meditation.
- Next, there is a short meditation on the event itself.
- This leads to an explanation of how that event in Jesus' life matches our own life, and how we can open that area of our life to God's healing love.
- A real-life illustration of this healing follows.
- Next, there is a prayerful reflection on how you can apply all this to your own life.
- Then say a decade of Hail Marys.
- The section closes with a brief prayer that can be said with the bead between decades. This prayer may be said after the Our Father and before the beginning of the next decade.

HOW TO PRAY THE ROSARY
FOR HEALING

The Rosary is a pattern of prayer that helps us to meditate more deeply on the life of Christ. We pray the Rosary by holding a rosary and saying a prayer for each bead. The spaces between the beads become spaces for silence and meditation.

There are many different ways to pray the Rosary, and different customs and prayers have grown up in different cultures and for different individuals.

Some people kneel to pray the Rosary, but to pray the Healing Rosary I recommend sitting comfortably, perhaps with a candle burning before an icon or a crucifix.

Most people begin by holding the crucifix and reciting the Apostles' Creed. This is followed by reciting the Lord's Prayer (Our Father) and three Hail Marys and a Glory Be on the beads that connect the crucifix to the main circlet of beads. When you get to the medal that joins these two groups of beads, I recommend that you stop and ask God to use this prayer for your healing. You may use your own form of words or you might like to say,

> By the power of this Rosary, I pray the Blessed Virgin Mary to intercede for me for my healing, the healing of my family, and the healing of the world. This I ask by the redemption won for us by the suffering, death, and resurrection of the one Lord, Jesus Christ. Amen.

Pope John Paul recommended beginning each decade by announcing the mystery for that decade and, taking a moment, holding the chain before the decade of beads to visualize the events of this particular mystery. In this book, you will find material to help you visualize the event and apply it to your personal needs. After that, pray the decade slowly, allowing the Lord's healing to be applied to your situation.

You may feel that God is doing wonderful things as you pray through a particular mystery. Maybe you feel he is bringing up many things that need to be dealt with. If so, take your time. Allow the Holy Spirit to work through your life at that point. You may feel that you want to repeat that mystery. That's good. You may feel that you want to stop and simply rest in God's healing presence and not complete the entire sequence of mysteries. That's fine. Be led by the Spirit, and allow him to guide your prayer.

You may feel that the meditations designed for healing don't apply to your situation. In that case, please still pray the Rosary for healing, but allow your prayers to be focused on other people you know who are in the situation I describe. If you do not know people who are in that situation, please pray for the healing of those unknown to you, for the healing of your community and the healing of the world.

Many people have doubts, questions, and fears about the healing ministry. We worry that God won't answer our prayers, that we will look foolish because the person wasn't healed after all. Don't worry too much about this. When I began to work in the healing ministry, I expressed such doubts to an old priest with whom I was working. I said, "What if we lay hands on a person and pray and nothing happens?" He smiled and said, "Oh, something always happens!"

So it is with praying the Rosary for healing. Don't worry. Something always happens! It's just that it is not for us to say what God will do. If we pray faithfully, he will be faithful in keeping his promises. How and when he keeps his promises is his business! All we have to do is watch and wait, and eventually we will see the power of his healing love in our world.

I

❖

The Joyful Mysteries

ANNUNCIATION
Conception

In the sixth month the angel Gabriel was sent from God to a city of Galilee named Nazareth, to a virgin betrothed to a man whose name was Joseph, of the house of David; and the virgin's name was Mary. And he came to her and said, "Hail, full of grace, the Lord is with you!" But she was greatly troubled at the saying, and considered in her mind what sort of greeting this might be. And the angel said to her, "Do not be afraid, Mary, for you have found favor with God. And behold, you will conceive in your womb and bear a son, and you shall call his name Jesus.

He will be great, and will be called the Son of the Most High;
and the Lord God will give to him the throne of his father David,
and he will reign over the house of Jacob for ever;
and of his kingdom there will be no end."

And Mary said to the angel, "How can this be, since I have no husband?" And the angel said to her,

"The Holy Spirit will come upon you,
and the power of the Most High will overshadow you;
therefore the child to be born will be called holy,
the Son of God.

And behold, your kinswoman Elizabeth in her old age has also conceived a son; and this is the sixth month with her who was called barren. For with God nothing will be impossible." And Mary said, "Behold, I am the handmaid of the Lord; let it be to me according to your word." And the angel departed from her.

LUKE 1:26-38

A beautiful girl is overshadowed by the angel of God and says a simple "yes." At that moment, the God-man is conceived. It is a moment the whole of humanity has been waiting for. In that one instant, a new kind of humanity is created, and the course of history is changed forever. In that moment of affirmation, the love of God and the potential of mankind meet. As the child is conceived, all that the man Jesus will be and do is held in a pure concentrated form of one cell charged with God's power and love. This is a moment of pure and perfect creation. The abundance of God bursts into human form in all glory, simplicity, and power.

Think It Through

The moment of our own conception was the foundation moment of our life. Many people believe the conditions of our conception actually influence our personality and the course of our later development. If we were conceived in love, security, warmth, tenderness, and the sacramental grace of marriage, then the foundation of our life is one of love, security, confidence, tenderness, energy, and grace.

Unfortunately, not all of us were conceived in this situation. No matter how wonderful our parents were, they too were locked into the curse of original sin. Within the act of making love they brought their own failures, selfishness, lack of love, and imperfections. As we share all their genetic characteristics, so we also share their intangible character traits. These aspects of our parents became incarnate in us as they made love and we were conceived. At that moment, all the good and bad characteristics of both parents fused in one explosive moment of creation. It was that moment in which we were conceived, and the foundation of our lives was established.

Each union of man and woman has the potential to create a new life. If the union was full of love, mercy, tenderness, and total self-giving, then the child conceived has a positive foundation of his or her being. If, however, the sexual union was negative, it is possible that the negativities will be at the foundation of the child's life.

If we were conceived outside marriage, or in a moment of immature or drunken lust, then these negative elements may be at the foundation of our being. The English psychiatrist Frank Lake did some groundbreaking work forty years ago, and he claimed that the moment of our conception did indeed influence the later development of our lives. He theorized that if we were conceived in an act of rebellion, rage, or violence, then violence, rebellion, and rage would be grounded in the foundation of our personality. If this is true, then these dark elements at the very foundation of our lives will continue to haunt us and terrify us. The negative foundation may lead to mysterious compulsions and addictive behaviors that seem to have no cure.

Healing Example

As a priest, I was once asked to counsel a young man named David. At the age of fifteen, David suddenly developed an irrationally rebellious streak. This was combined with an obsession with cars, and he had already been caught stealing cars for joyriding. His parents were at their wits' end. In talking to them, we discovered that David had been adopted, and that he had been conceived when his mother was fifteen, in the backseat of a car. We had a Mass of Reconciliation, in which David (by God's grace) forgave his birth parents. His irrational behavior stopped immediately, and real harmony was established with his adoptive family.

Pray for Healing

As we meditate on the perfect conception of Jesus at the Annunciation, any negativity or absence of love in our lives at the moment of our own conception can be made up by the radiant love of God expressed at the moment of the conception of Jesus. As you meditate on the events of Jesus' conception, imagine the total purity of Mary. Can you see her youthful beauty and the rapture of her total love for God? Can you experience the surge of power and love that God poured into her? Can you open yourself to that same healing, life-giving power? Can you feel the way that Mary was "full of grace?" That fullness was the fullness and totality of God's love being poured into that moment of the creation of new life.

Now let the Holy Spirit move you back to the moment of your own conception. You cannot remember that moment, but can you imagine it? Can you place yourself in the amazingly tiny state of a seed and egg meeting? You were once just two cells at the creation point of a new life. Allow the Holy Spirit to bring you to that simple moment of life. Can you feel what the emotion was like at that moment in time? Was it full of love, tenderness, and God's grace, or was there negativity, lust, or rage within that foundation moment? Was there tension, selfishness, and fear? Was there a lack of trust, despair, or anger?

Let it go. Let Jesus Christ's forgiveness and healing into that moment. Feel God's perfect fatherly love and grace filling that moment. Allow the motherly love of Mary to overwhelm any gaps and failings in the love of your human parents. Allow the forgiveness of Christ to flow to them. He loves them and knows their failings. He knows all the gaps in their lives too. Take time. Allow Christ's healing love to seep into every tiny crevice at the very beginnings and foundation of your personality.

Rest in the knowledge and presence of Jesus Christ the healer. He is there at that moment. You were formed in his perfect love. You are safe, secure, loved, and valued. You are infinitely precious in his sight.

Thank God for This Gift

Heavenly Father, you have created me in your own image. Heal any wounds and forgive any sins that may have surrounded the moment of my conception, and by the Holy Spirit continue to create in me a new heart each day. This I ask through Christ my Lord. Amen.

VISITATION
Gestation

In those days Mary arose and went with haste into the hill country, to a city of Judah, and she entered the house of Zechariah and greeted Elizabeth. And when Elizabeth heard the greeting of Mary, the babe leaped in her womb; and Elizabeth was filled with the Holy Spirit and she exclaimed with a loud cry, "Blessed are you among women, and blessed is the fruit of your womb! And why is this granted me, that the mother of my Lord should come to me? For behold, when the voice of your greeting came to my ears, the babe in my womb leaped for joy. And blessed is she who believed that there would be a fulfilment of what was spoken to her from the Lord." And Mary said,

> *"My soul magnifies the Lord,*
> *and my spirit rejoices in God my Savior,*
> *for he has regarded the low estate of his handmaiden.*
> *For behold, henceforth all generations will call me blessed;*
> *for he who is mighty has done great things for me,*
> *and holy is his name.*
> *And his mercy is on those who fear him*
> *from generation to generation.*
> *He has shown strength with his arm,*
> *he has scattered the proud in the imagination of their hearts,*
> *he has put down the mighty from their thrones,*
> *and exalted those of low degree;*
> *he has filled the hungry with good things,*
> *and the rich he has sent empty away.*
> *He has helped his servant Israel,*
> *in remembrance of his mercy,*

as he spoke to our fathers,
to Abraham and to his posterity for ever."

And Mary remained with her about three months, and returned
to her home.

LUKE 1:39-56

The pregnant girl travels to visit her older cousin, who is also
pregnant. Both women are full of joy and wonder at the
miracles God has done in their lives. As they share their stories,
the children in their wombs recognize each other. One child
leaps for joy. Both women laugh with delight and sing the
praise of God. Both women are secure in their faith and hope
in God. The young woman is especially blessed. She is totally
full of God's grace, and she nurtures her Son with a totality of
love and perfection. As he grows in her womb, he knows
absolute love, unconditional acceptance, and the fullness of
God's grace present in his mother's life. This is a moment of
natural joy infused with God's power, grace, and total goodness.

Think It Through

The nine months in our mother's womb was a time of development and growth. The foundation experiences of our life
were laid down as our bodies and minds took their form. If our
time in the womb was full of peace, comfort, security, and
grace, then these powerfully positive elements were woven into
our developing personality. If our mother experienced joy,
peace, and love as she carried us, these emotions were trans-
ferred to us. If she carried us within an atmosphere of ease,
security, faith, and beauty, then the joy she experienced in this

wonderful time of gestation came through to us and became a foundational part of our personality.

If, however, the time in our mother's womb was negative in any way, then the negativities were also woven into the formation of our lives. The negativity could have been illness or stress. Perhaps our mother was overworked, tired, and worried. Maybe our mother had mixed emotions about her pregnancy and wasn't sure she really wanted us. These emotions came through and made up part of our personality.

It could be that the time we spent in the womb was very negative. Some mothers smoke, drink, and take drugs during a pregnancy, and these negative behaviors affect the unborn child. The father may be absent or a negative influence. Family and friends may produce a negative atmosphere during the pregnancy. All these things are communicated and registered in the unborn child's development.

It can be even worse. A mother may hate the child she has conceived. She may even try to kill the child.

Healing Example

A middle-aged woman named Alice came to see me for counseling. During her whole life, Alice had been subject to two irrational fears: choking to death and having her throat cut. She was in a terrible state because she had developed a growth in her throat that was slowly choking her to death, and the only option was surgery in which she would have to have her throat cut.

We prayed with her, and the priest I was working with asked her to think about her early childhood. The next week she returned saying that an aunt she hadn't heard from for years telephoned to talk to her. The aunt said she felt compelled to tell Alice that when her mother was pregnant she had tried to abort her — first by holding her breath, then with a sharp knife. This had happened in November. Alice's phobias were always worst in November. We had a Healing Mass for Alice, in which she forgave her now dead mother. The next week Alice had another x-ray, and the growth in her throat was gone.

Pray for Healing

As you meditate on the visitation of Mary to Elizabeth, share the joy of the two pregnant women. Visualize the fullness of their feminine beauty in the midst of pregnancy. Concentrate on the youthful beauty and flush of joy in Mary's face and eyes. This shows the fullness of beauty, grace, and faith that accompanies a perfect pregnancy. All of this beauty, trust, power, and confidence was being communicated to Mary's child. For nine months, Jesus was formed in the womb of the perfect mother. By God's grace, Mary was able to offer the developing child totally full and overwhelming acceptance and unconditional love.

Now allow the Holy Spirit to take your mind and memory back to the nine months within your own mother's womb. This may be a good memory, full of happiness, peace, and love. However, you may also feel stresses and strains. You may remember vague emotions of fear and anxiety, or anger and frustration. Your mother may have gone through some crisis during your pregnancy. There may have been illness, complications, or circumstances of violence or distress. During those nine months, there may have been external problems for your mother — family matters or difficulties with relationships may have caused stress and tension and pain. Can you feel the emotions of this time? What was it like for you?

Let it go. Let Jesus Christ heal any negative parts of those first nine months of life. Let the negative emotions be swamped by the power of Mary's perfect motherhood. At the cross, Jesus says to us: "Here is your mother" (see Jn 19:27). Whatever was lacking in your own formation in the womb, Mary, through God's grace, will make up the difference. Allow her motherly love to touch you and complete your formation. Allow your brother Jesus to minister his healing love to you. Know the security and total acceptance of God the Father.

Rest in the presence of Jesus Christ the healer. Allow him to complete the healing over time as you go about your day's work. If any negative emotions or experiences from your time in the womb are brought to mind, simply take them to confession. Don't go into detail. Just say, "I confess the pain and stresses of my early life and ask for the forgiveness and healing of Christ."

Thank God for This Gift

Father in heaven, through the prayers of St. Elizabeth and the Blessed Virgin Mary, may any hurt or trauma I experienced in the womb be healed, may anyone who injured me be forgiven, and may I grow forever in the knowledge of your love. This I ask through Christ my Lord. Amen.

NATIVITY
Birth

In those days a decree went out from Caesar Augustus that all the world should be enrolled. This was the first enrollment, when Quirinius was governor of Syria. And all went to be enrolled, each to his own city. And Joseph also went up from Galilee, from the city of Nazareth, to Judea, to the city of David, which is called Bethlehem, because he was of the house and lineage of David, to be enrolled with Mary his betrothed, who was with child. And while they were there, the time came for her to be delivered. And she gave birth to her first-born son and wrapped him in swaddling cloths, and laid him in a manger, because there was no place for them in the inn. And in that region there were shepherds out in the field, keeping watch over their flock by night. And an angel of the Lord appeared to them, and the glory of the Lord shone around them, and they were filled with fear. And the angel said to them, "Be not afraid; for behold, I bring you good news of a great joy which will come to all the people; for to you is born this day in the city of David a Savior, who is Christ the Lord. And this will be a sign for you: you will find a baby wrapped in swaddling cloths and lying in a manger." And suddenly there was with the angel a multitude of the heavenly host praising God and saying,

> *"Glory to God in the highest,*
> *and on earth peace among men with whom he is pleased!"*

When the angels went away from them into heaven, the shepherds said to one another, "Let us go over to Bethlehem and see this thing that has happened, which the Lord has made known to us." And they went with haste, and found Mary and Joseph, and the baby lying in a manger. And when they saw it they made known the saying which had been told them concerning this child; and all who heard it wondered at what the shepherds told them. But Mary kept all these things, pondering them in her heart. And the shepherds returned, glorifying and praising God for all they had heard and seen, as it had been told them.

LUKE 2:1-20

Mary and Joseph have made the journey to Bethlehem, and Mary's child is about to be born. The stable is probably a cave in the hill behind a simple inn. The ancient legends suggest that a local woman comes to help with the birth, and that the miraculous birth of Jesus Christ is without the usual pain of childbirth. The gospel doesn't tell us this, but if Mary was, by God's grace, kept from original sin, then she would have been spared the pain of childbirth, which is part of the curse of sin. If this is so, can you see the pure delight at this birth? Can you share the wonder and joy in the eyes of Mary and Joseph at the birth of this perfect infant? In one sense, it is as simple and natural as any birth. At the same time, God himself is born into the world in a moment of total joy, peace, and beauty.

Think It Through

The time in our mother's womb came to a sudden end one day. The contractions started and we were expelled naked into a bright, noisy, and cold world. If the experience was peaceful, confident, and full of love, then our entrance into the world was the best it could be. This first experience of life became another foundation block for the rest of our life.

Even with the best circumstances, however, the experience was traumatic. We were thrust from a world of comfort, security, and warmth to a world that must have seemed cold, harsh, loud, and bright. If our birth was complicated with other negative factors, it could have been a very difficult and negative foundation block for our later life.

Our birth might have been complicated through medical factors. Maybe it was a breech birth or an otherwise difficult labor. Maybe we were born by cesarean section and the birth was therefore unnatural. Maybe we were born prematurely and our first experience of life was in intensive care. It could be that we were adopted, and that part of our birth experience was being removed from our mother and handed to our adoptive parents. It is possible that our mother was depressed or unable to really love and accept us fully. Maybe we were injured in the birth process or traumatized in some way. Whatever happened, our birth experience was our first meeting with the stress and pain of real life, and this first experience of life became a foundation block of our later life.

Healing Example

Sometimes the problems that come up later are mysteriously symbolic of what happened in the birth experience. When I was involved in counseling with another priest, we met a young man in his twenties named Philip. Philip was intelligent and well educated, but he was unable to really get started in his adult life. He tried to make commitments and tried to get a job, but somehow he was stuck. When we asked him how he would describe his problem he said, "It's like I'm stuck in a rut and can't get out. When I try to get started with a job or a relationship, I get panic attacks and back off."

As our relationship developed, we asked Philip to ask his mother what his birth was like. The next meeting was very emotional. His mother had described how his birth was a breech birth. He had tried to turn in the birth canal and got stuck. One arm emerged, only to be pulled back. The doctors tried to turn him. There was an atmosphere of panic in the delivery room. Philip's mother was terrified that the baby would have brain damage, and only at the last moment were the doctors able to turn him for the safe delivery. We helped Philip bring these memories to Christ, and in time he was able to work through his fears, eventually creating a successful marriage and career.

Pray for Healing

Can you see the events surrounding the birth of Jesus Christ? The cave stable was probably snug and warm. With straw on the floor and soft lamp light, it was a perfect place to be born. God saw fit that, despite the poor surroundings, his Son was born into a place of quiet warmth, the sweet smell of hay mingling with the earthy smell of the animals. The infant was welcomed into the world by the most beautiful smiling face you can imagine — the face of the Virgin Mary. The first sounds he heard were the friendly sounds of the animals and the deep voice of his loving earthly father, Joseph.

Now let the Holy Spirit take you back to your own birth. Maybe there was trauma of some kind. There might have been anxiety, fear, or danger. Was there anything negative? There was the pain of childbirth and the natural anxiety all mothers must feel. Was there any other trauma, distress, or danger?

Let God take any pain or trauma from your birth experience and heal it through the perfect birth of Jesus Christ at Bethlehem. Allow the pain and trauma of childbirth to be taken away. Let any distress or danger, fear or anxiety, be swept away in the loving confidence of St. Joseph and the totally unconditional love of Mary, your Mother. Allow yourself to be "born again" in this way, and have any gaps completed and fulfilled.

Rest in the healing love of Christ, and allow the Holy Spirit to work this healing through your whole life over time. Pray for mothers and children going through childbirth at this time. And if this meditation has unlocked any trauma or pain from your experience of birth, take it to confession and simply say, "I confess the damage done to me through my earliest experiences and ask for Christ's healing and forgiveness."

Thank God for This Gift

Heavenly Father, by the perfect birth of your Son, Jesus Christ, in Bethlehem, heal the pain of my own birth and lead me to be born again in the power of the Holy Spirit. Amen.

PRESENTATION IN
THE TEMPLE
Childhood

And when the time came for their purification according to the law of Moses, they brought him up to Jerusalem to present him to the Lord (as it is written in the law of the Lord, "Every male that opens the womb shall be called holy to the Lord") and to offer a sacrifice according to what is said in the law of the Lord, "a pair of turtledoves, or two young pigeons." Now there was a man in Jerusalem, whose name was Simeon, and this man was righteous and devout, looking for the consolation of Israel, and the Holy Spirit was upon him. And it had been revealed to him by the Holy Spirit that he should not see death before he had seen the Lord's Christ. And inspired by the Spirit he came into the temple; and when the parents brought in the child Jesus, to do for him according to the custom of the law, he took him up in his arms and blessed God and said,

> *"Lord, now let your servant depart in peace,*
> *according to your word;*
> *for my eyes have seen your salvation*
> *which you have prepared in the presence of all peoples,*
> *a light for revelation to the Gentiles,*
> *and for glory to your people Israel."*

And his father and his mother marveled at what was said about him; and Simeon blessed them and said to Mary his mother,

> *"Behold, this child is set for the fall and rising of many in Israel,*
> *and for a sign that is spoken against*
> *(and a sword will pierce through your own soul also),*
> *that thoughts out of many hearts may be revealed."*

And there was a prophetess, Anna, the daughter of Phanuel, of the tribe of Asher; she was of a great age, having lived with her husband seven years from her virginity, and as a widow till she was eighty-four. She did not depart from the temple, worshiping with fasting and prayer night and day. And coming up at that very hour she gave thanks to God, and spoke of him to all who were looking for the redemption of Jerusalem.

And when they had performed everything according to the law of the Lord, they returned into Galilee, to their own city, Nazareth.

LUKE 2:22-39

Within the first few days of his birth, Joseph and Mary take the newborn child to be presented in the Temple. This is a ritual similar to infant baptism or dedicating a child to God. The young woman is full of simple joy and pride as she goes with her husband to the Temple. There they meet Simeon and Anna — an old man and an old woman whose lives are dedicated to prayer and the service of God. The ancient legends suggest that Mary may have served in the Temple as a dedicated child, and that she already knows Simeon and Anna. The four of them — the mother, the foster father, and the old man and woman — welcome the child into the family of God, and through the ritual offering, the boy's childhood begins with God's perfect blessing and a family full of acceptance and love.

Think It Through

Our infancy and childhood years are times of exploration, innocence, and joy. As we grow, we discover marvelous things about the world around us. Day by day we learn more about the world. We learn to listen and speak, and we learn to walk and run. Eventually, we go to school and take on an incredible amount of information and experience. It is a time of wonder, openness, fun, and joyful play. We also learn how to accept and return love. In a loving home, we receive unconditional love from our family, and we return that love with willing obedience and the simple pleasure of pleasing our parents. These simple experiences become the vocabulary of love for later life. In our first fourteen years, we learn how to live life. We learn how to love. We learn the basics of everything that will follow.

However, if things go wrong in the first years of life, much more will go wrong later. As we move through childhood, a whole range of things can go wrong. We may suffer illness or injury. We may be in a family that cannot or will not accept and love us fully. Through our own willfulness and disobedience, we may cut ourselves off from others. In later childhood, we can start to make wrong choices and indulge in conscious and deliberate sin, and this can establish a pattern of behavior that is hard to change. Childhood is meant to be a time of innocent enjoyment, wonder, and joy. When things go wrong in childhood, they usually go very wrong.

If there is abuse in the family, the child's development is distorted and twisted. If there is physical abuse, the child learns to equate violence with love. If there is sexual abuse, the child's ability to develop a natural sexuality may be ruined forever. If there is mental abuse, the child's perception of sanity and normal behavior is destroyed. If there is emotional abuse, the child's ability to love and be loved is wrecked. If there is spiritual abuse, the child receives a distorted and perverted understanding of religion and God's love. It is almost impossible to come through childhood without some kind of trauma or injury that has lasting effects throughout the rest of our lives.

Healing Example

I remember meeting Sonya — a painfully thin girl in her early twenties. Sonya had poor posture, kept her head down, and wore her hair with long bangs that nearly covered her face. She was finding it hard to find a job because she had been expelled from school. When I asked what she had been expelled for, she said: "Whenever I walked to or from school, I broke the milk bottles on people's doorsteps. Then when I broke a window at school, they kicked me out." Sonya was famous for breaking windows. She broke lots of windows.

I asked Sonya why she broke the bottles and the windows. She didn't know. I asked her to look at me and said, "Did you break the glass because there was a fragile little girl who was broken once?" I then heard the story of how a trusted Christian pastor and family friend had sexually abused Sonya on a regular basis from the age of seven. After we had a Mass of Forgiveness for Sonya, she started to stand up straight and tall. She got a job, and a few years later she got married and started a family. She gave up breaking bottles and windows.

Pray for Healing

Can you see Joseph and Mary presenting the infant Christ to God and asking for his blessing and protection? This presentation in the Temple was the beginning of Jesus' childhood. God was asked to receive the child and to bless his growth, learning, and development. We don't know much about Jesus' childhood years, but we do know that he developed within a perfectly loving family, and that he submitted to his teachers and parents. He must have been a perfect child, in the sense that every step of his development was full, abundant, loving, and free. Because he got all the support he needed, he must have been confident without being arrogant, and humble without being subservient. Can you see the boy Jesus? He wasn't especially pious or outstandingly "holy." He was all that a boy should be — natural, happy, inquisitive, loving, joyful, and free.

Can you allow the Holy Spirit to take you back to your own childhood? Were you brought up in a Christian family? Were you baptized as an infant? If so, God began his work of grace in you at that point. Can you thank God for this wonderful grace, and see that he is still working in your life?

Let your mind go back to your childhood years. Does the Spirit bring to mind anything that was painful, traumatic, or abusive? Were there things you chose to do that you knew were wrong, which you have never asked forgiveness for? Are there relationships that went wrong? Were there people who disappointed you? Did anyone hurt you? Were there any instances of violence, sexual abuse, or mental, emotional, or spiritual abuse? The result of these things in adult life is a lack of joy, depression, inability to make good, loving relationships, and a failure to grow spiritually. The result of a bad childhood is an inability to trust, which surfaces as a cynical, suspicious, and angry spirit.

Can you picture the child Jesus? Can you see his wholeness, his joy, and his freedom? If you suffered any pain, trauma, or abuse, let him take it. Let Jesus Christ's perfect childhood complement yours and lift from you the memories of any trauma, abuse, or suffering. If your childhood was wrecked by anxiety, abuse, illness, or injury, allow Jesus Christ to restore the child within. Ask Jesus to heal the injuries and wounds of childhood, and to forgive anyone who harmed you. Jesus said that unless you become as a little child, you cannot enter the kingdom. Ask Jesus Christ to restore the child within you, and to grant you joy, innocence, simplicity, and the freedom to trust.

If childhood abuse was regular and repeated, you may need regular and repeated forgiveness and healing. You may need to come back to this time and again to find the healing of Christ. Don't worry if it takes time. Don't worry if you have to come back again to ask for healing. If the injury was repeated, the healing and forgiveness may need to be repeated. Give the recovery time. Give the healing time. If there are sins from your childhood that you have never confessed, take them simply to confession. If others have harmed you in childhood, take it to confession.

Thank God for This Gift

Father God, heal all that went wrong in my child-hood. Complete all that was lacking. Forgive all my sins and the sins of those who harmed me. Through the perfect childhood of your Son, Jesus Christ, and by the power of the Holy Spirit, restore the child in me so that I will be able to trust in your father-like care with simple, child-like trust. Amen.

FINDING IN THE TEMPLE
Adolescence

And when he was twelve years old, they went up according to custom; and when the feast was ended, as they were returning, the boy Jesus stayed behind in Jerusalem. His parents did not know it, but supposing him to be in the company they went a day's journey, and they sought him among their kinsfolk and acquaintances; and when they did not find him, they returned to Jerusalem, seeking him. After three days they found him in the temple, sitting among the teachers, listening to them and asking them questions; and all who heard him were amazed at his understanding and his answers. And when they saw him they were astonished; and his mother said to him, "Son, why have you treated us so? Behold, your father and I have been looking for you anxiously." And he said to them, "How is it that you sought me? Did you not know that I must be in my Father's house?" And they did not understand the saying which he spoke to them. And he went down with them and came to Nazareth, and was obedient to them; and his mother kept all these things in her heart.

And Jesus increased in wisdom and in stature, and in favor with God and man.

LUKE 2:42-52

When a child is lost, everyone panics. The child becomes distressed and the parents become increasingly frantic looking for the child. When he is found, all is forgiven in the joy. The young mother and her husband look everywhere for their Son, only to find him seated in the Temple precincts discussing theology and Scripture with the teachers and wise men. At the age of twelve, Jesus passes from boyhood into adolescence, and he answers them with respectful confidence: "Didn't you realize I would be in my Father's house?" Already he has a clear sense of vocation and mission. Despite his youth, he knows where he is going in life and how to steer through the difficult maze of growing up.

Think It Through

As we pass from childhood to adolescence, we enter a turbulent time when we are faced with extraordinary new pressures. Hormones push our bodies into adulthood while our emotions race to catch up. We face a whole range of challenges that force us to move from the freedom and innocence of childhood into the complexity of being adults. We are given new freedoms, but we are also faced with daunting new responsibilities. Peer pressure builds, and the new challenges can cause our confidence to crumble. Confusing new temptations arise. It's easy to lose our way, confuse our priorities, and develop destructive new habits. With a strong faith, a loving family, and good friends and mentors, adolescence can be a time for life-changing choices, positive actions, and the springboard to an abundant, prosperous, and mature adulthood.

However, adolescence can also be a disaster. The new challenges, temptations, and responsibilities can simply overwhelm us. Even with a good family, wrong friends and a few bad choices can endanger our whole future, harm others, and turn us onto the path of destruction. Adolescence is a dramatic time when we make important decisions, and begin to pay the price. The way of the world becomes vividly real, and the attractions of sin, the flesh, and the devil lure us away from the narrow way of the abundant life Christ promises.

Our own choices can divert us down the wrong path in adolescence, but the rest of our path is also riddled with minefields. Friends who are already on the wrong path can lead us astray. Negative family patterns start to surface and re-echo into horrible conflict. Adolescents can find themselves driven by the same demons that haunted their parents. Our instincts are to be independent of our parents — but this natural drive can turn into rebellion, and problems with our parents can take root in bitterness and resentment. In adolescence, we realize that adults we trusted are frail human beings. Our idealism and faith can be shattered as a result. Added to this, the abuse of adolescents happens all the time. Those in positions of trust abuse vulnerable young people physically, sexually, mentally, emotionally, and spiritually. The results are disastrous, with the young person drifting into cynicism, despair, rebellion, addiction, and even suicide.

Healing Example

I met Paul at the gym. In his mid-thirties, he looked really fit. Paul was a sports fanatic and fitness coach. He was also a drug addict and alcoholic. When he helped me train, he began to tell his story.

When he was a boy, his parents split up. At age twelve, he witnessed his alcoholic father attempt suicide. When he was nineteen, he was called to identify his father's broken body at the base of a tall building. Paul told me how he started drinking and sniffing glue with friends in junior high school. It made him feel stronger and more able to cope. By high school, he was selling drugs and getting stoned every weekend. By his twenties, he had a string of failed relationships behind him and had helped two of his girlfriends get abortions. Now in his mid-thirties, he was going through a divorce, and trying to be a father to his only son. Despite all attempts to stay clean, he still went out on regular binges. First he would get drunk; then he would go out to find the drugs. He knew addicts and the world of addiction. He saw that he was headed for the gutter, but he couldn't help himself. The patterns of behavior had been established in adolescence, and he couldn't get out of them.

Our relationship shifted. He was helping me get physically fit. He then asked me to help him get spiritually fit. We went to a priest who was able to help. He celebrated a Healing Mass for Paul, prayed for the soul of Paul's father, and helped to bury all the ghosts of the past. Paul says that from that moment he felt a breakthrough. He still has his guard up against alcohol and drugs, but he's been clean now for two years.

Pray for Healing

Can you see Jesus as a twelve year old, and then as a handsome young teenager? He was the perfect son, learning from his elders, yet challenging them with the zeal, idealism, and joy of youth. If he was perfect, then a good sense of humor and fun balanced his seriousness and sensitivity. Like every adolescent, he must have been full of curiosity, questions, energy, and joy. With a perfect mother and a mature and caring father, Jesus' adolescence was a time for growth, learning, and a deepening love for his heavenly Father. From his mother, Mary, he observed and practiced a deep purity — not a falsely pious and negative purity, but a wholesome, full, and positive purity. The youthful Jesus had a confident sense of his own destiny, and he had already discovered his vocation. He understood the right priorities and ran on the path of perfection, his heart overflowing with love and a full, abundant, and joyful spirit.

Can you remember your own adolescence? Were you happy and trusting, or were you confused, insecure, and anxious? What was your relationship with your parents like? Did you enjoy your family life? What were your friends like? Did you go through your teenage years making the right choices in simple hope for the future, or did you follow a path of rebellion, selfishness, and lack of responsibility? Did anyone abuse you when you were a teenager? Sexual abuse happens too often, but emotional, mental, and spiritual abuses are even more commonplace. Emotional, mental, and spiritual abuses occur when young people are pressured, blackmailed, and coerced into incorrect behaviors against their will and choice. While they are vulnerable, they are violated by adults who hold all the power. Did you make wrong choices and start patterns of destructive behavior to which you are still addicted? Addictions to drugs, drink, food, pornography, and distorted sexual practices can all begin in adolescence. You can be free of all these chains.

Picture the twelve-year-old Jesus in the Temple. He is bright-eyed, intelligent, happy, and free. Go with him as he grows up over the next years of his life. Do you see how he grows into a confident, strong, and handsome young man? See how his vocation gives meaning to his whole life. It gives him focus. It gives him energy. It gives him freedom to love and be loved. Now shadow him within your own memories of adolescence. Let his perfect growth and maturity correct what went wrong for you. See how his relationship with his parents is loving, yet he is naturally independent of them. See how he avoids the negative choices — not out of fear, but out of a love for all that is good, beautiful, and free. Make those choices with him.

See how he prays, and notice how he is learning to walk with God and discern his vocation. Splice these growing points into the memories of your own adolescence and be healed.

The young Jesus also sees the sins in your life at that stage. He understands the roots of those sins and forgives you. He also sees the abuse you suffered, the confusion you felt, and the pain you experienced. He wants to take all the darkness, forgive you, and set you free to enter into the fullness of his abundant life.

If your life went seriously off track at this stage, you may need to return to this part of the Healing Rosary and spend more time allowing God to heal the wounds, forgive the sins, and cleanse the memories. Throughout his adolescence, Jesus' mother was always there. She shared his doubts and fears and difficult choices with him. She now ministers in heaven to go through your healing with you. Spend time realizing her presence, and ask for her healing help and prayer. If there was serious sin from this time in your life that has never been taken to confession, now is the time to do it. You don't need to go into lots of detail. Simply state the sin in an objective and precise way and ask forgiveness. If you were abused or hurt by others during this stage of your life, bring that to confession too. Simply confess that you were abused, and ask for healing and for the power to forgive the abuser.

❖
Thank God for This Gift

Father in heaven, like the prodigal son, I am returning to the comfort and power of your love. Forgive all that went wrong in my adolescent years. I didn't know what I was doing. By the perfect youth and manhood of Jesus Christ, restore and redeem my youth. Make it a time of confidence and joy, purity and power. Grant this through the mighty work of the Holy Spirit, and with the prayers of Mary, ever-Virgin and ever my Mother. Amen.

II

❖

The Luminous
Mysteries

BAPTISM IN THE JORDAN
Vocation and Early Adulthood

And when Jesus was baptized, he went up immediately from the water, and behold, the heavens were opened and he saw the Spirit of God descending like a dove, and alighting on him; and behold, a voice from heaven, saying, "This is my beloved Son, with whom I am well pleased."

MATTHEW 3:16-17

The crowd has gathered by the riverside to listen to the preacher, when suddenly he stops. Another young man steps from the crowd and moves forward to be baptized. The people are speechless. Somehow this man moves and behaves with total confidence, authority, and simplicity. In the midst of their confusion, weakness, and fear, this man moves with clarity of purpose, strength, and courage. They hear how this new preacher recently read from the Scriptures in his local synagogue with a startling claim to the anointed one from God. He is a man with a mission, a man to be listened to, and a man who will transform lives and transform the world.

Think It Through

If we are lucky, as we move from adolescence into adulthood, we discover our vocation. A vocation is wonderful because it gives our lives direction. We know what we are here for. We have a purpose, a mission, a goal, and a dream. This dream drives everything we do. It helps us to be disciplined; it gives us a reason for study, hard work, and ambition. It helps us set priorities and order the loves of our life. Everything focuses down into the mission that we have been given, and we set off on the adventure of adult life with zeal, drive, and the extraordinary power of youth channeled into a purposeful goal.

At this stage of life, however, things often go terribly wrong. If we don't have a sense of vocation, we start to drift. We drift into relationships that go nowhere. We drift in and out of jobs that go nowhere. We drift in and out of all forms of entertainment and diversion — desperately seeking what we should do with our lives. If we are not careful, our aimless shiftlessness leads into sinful forms of entertainment and diversion. We can fall into addictive, escapist behaviors. We start to link up with other aimless, shiftless people and start into a nosedive that is difficult to pull out of. Sometimes, at this stage, we simply drift into a loveless marriage, or a boring and conventionally respectable life, but it is still a life without direction, a life without meaning, and a life without purpose.

A life without meaning and purpose eventually ends in lack of faith, cynicism, despair, and even suicide. If the beginning of our adult life lacked any sense of calling, purpose, or vocation, then the rest of our life also lacks purpose. In order to put this right, we may need to go back in our memory to our early adulthood and find where we went off the path and get back on the right way. This will require repentance, forgiveness, and healing.

Healing Example

Bernard was a man going through a midlife crisis. He was a successful vice president of a bank, with four children of high school and college age. His wife had been a loyal supporter for their twenty-two-year marriage, but they had drifted into marriage right out of college because they just thought it was what they were supposed to do. Bernard's wife, Nancy, was the one who came to talk. Bernard had confessed to an affair with a much younger woman. He had also recently bought a very expensive motorcycle and said he was going to drive to the West Coast with the younger woman and that he "needed time off."

After listening to Bernard, I discovered that he had once felt a vocation to be a missionary priest, but had denied the vocation and become a banker instead. When he went back to that youthful vision and was forgiven for neglecting it, he was able to make the right midlife re-start. Bernard took early retirement, and he and Nancy joined a short-term lay missionary team to Africa. When they returned, he joined the home team as a development officer, and in his later life found the vocation he had neglected for so long.

Pray for Healing

As you meditate on the baptism of Jesus, can you see the complete confidence and courage with which he stepped out into his public ministry? Here is a man who is totally sure of his calling, his purpose, and his meaning in life. Can you see it from the calm, but bright sparkle in his dark eyes? Can you see it in his upright and energetic posture? Can you see it in the spring in his step, in the way he speaks to others and motivates and inspires them simply by being with them?

This is the way a true vocation energizes and directs people's lives. It becomes the driving force in all they do. This is the way grace works in lives. The more it fills people, the more they are energized with divine power within them. Jesus displays the fullness of this divine energy in human form. Can you see this as he comes up out of the water, and the clouds part and a ray of light shines on him? Here is a person full of power, energy, and direction. He is one with God the Father and the Holy Spirit.

Can you remember your own transition years from adolescence to adulthood? It may be that you are in this stage of life now. This may be the time when you are getting ready to leave high school or college. You are wondering what to do with your life. What job should you do? Whom will you marry? Where will you live? Who are your friends?

Did you drift at this time? Did you wait for others to make decisions for you? Did you drift back into a dependent state on your parents or other careers? Did you drift into destructive relationships, destructive habits, or destructive and addictive behaviors? Maybe you simply drifted into a marriage or a job that seemed the easiest course, but wasn't really the thing you were called to. If this is the case, then your life ever since that time has really been shiftless and empty, hasn't it? Even if you've had financial success, and an outwardly successful marriage and family, your life still has no vocation, and ultimately very little meaning.

Now allow the powerful vocation of Jesus Christ to touch your life. When you were baptized, you entered into his life and into his baptism, and you took on a share in his vocation to redeem the world. At some point in your life, you had a dream. You wanted to do something significant, something good, something that would change the world — even if it was a very humble and simple change. What was it?

Can you imagine Jesus, coming up from his baptism, full of a sense of mission and purpose? Does he look at you? Listen carefully. Does he give you something to do? Does he give you an idea and a way to have a vocation in life? It may be something very simple, such as being the best mother or father you can possibly be. It may be something practical or something spiritual. If you ask for your vocation, it will be given to you.

Was this stage in your life a time when you developed bad habits, a low level of self-worth or a sense of cynicism and despair? Did you do anything that has never been confessed that you are ashamed of? Did you experiment with sin or indulge in destructive behaviors that you have never brought to confession? All these things may still cloud your vision, impede your sense of vocation, and cause hurt, stress, illness, and a kind of spiritual handicap in your life. Ask God to bring them to mind, and then take them to confession to experience real healing and forgiveness. Imagine and experience the waters of your own baptism, as the grace of God washes through your life and cleanses the early adult years, and gives you a renewed sense of vocation and purpose in life.

Thank God for This Gift

Heavenly Father, at his baptism the unity Jesus enjoyed with you and the Holy Spirit was on display for all to see. By the power of this unity, forgive and heal the dis-unity, chaos, and selfish blindness of my early adult life. Even now, renew my baptismal vocation to love and serve you with the precious time you have given me. Empower me with a new infilling of the Holy Spirit, and lead me on the path of total union with your everlasting love. Amen.

WEDDING AT CANA
Love and Marriage

On the third day there was a marriage at Cana in Galilee, and the mother of Jesus was there; Jesus also was invited to the marriage, with his disciples. When the wine failed, the mother of Jesus said to him, "They have no wine." And Jesus said to her, "O woman, what have you to do with me? My hour has not yet come." His mother said to the servants, "Do whatever he tells you." Now six stone jars were standing there, for the Jewish rites of purification, each holding twenty or thirty gallons. Jesus said to them, "Fill the jars with water." And they filled them up to the brim. He said to them, "Now draw some out, and take it to the steward of the feast." So they took it. When the steward of the feast tasted the water now become wine, and did not know where it came from (though the servants who had drawn the water knew), the steward of the feast called the bridegroom and said to him, "Every man serves the good wine first; and when men have drunk freely, then the poor wine; but you have kept the good wine until now." This, the first of his signs, Jesus did at Cana in Galilee, and manifested his glory; and his disciples believed in him.

JOHN 2:1-11

In ancient times, Jewish wedding celebrations could last for days. Can you see Jesus arriving with his mother and a few of his disciples? The feasting has started and their arrival is almost unnoticed in the noisy party atmosphere. The wine has begun to run out, and there is a furtive conversation among the servants. Mary asks her Son to help. Is she asking for a miracle or simply for him to run an errand to get some wine from another supply?

He responds immediately. Quietly and confidently he produces an unexpected, supernatural supply of wine for the marriage feast. The feast goes on, seemingly unaffected, but now there is a new kind of wine filling all those who celebrate.

Think It Through

Marriage is the summit of the beautiful sexual instincts God has created within us. Through adolescence and early adulthood, these instincts are driving us toward a relationship that will complete us and help bring us to our full human potential. Through marriage, a man and a woman grow together and produce the fruit of their relationship — children who are each a unique fusion of that man and woman. St. Paul calls marriage a "mystery," and in the Christian life a "mystery" is a living truth that we must experience rather than explain. The experience of the marriage mystery takes us into the mystery of our relationship with God. The New Testament says that we are the bride and Christ is the bridegroom, and that our union with him is like a sacred marriage.

It is no wonder that this area of our lives is under constant attack by the devil. Instead of the exciting adventure of marriage, we pursue a range of cheap and degrading alternatives. We embark on shallow sexual adventures that damage other people and cloud our own spiritual vision. We get bogged down in the swamp of pornography, lust, shallow fantasies, and selfish pleasure. This leads to spiritual lethargy and a perverted perspective on love and the meaning of life. As a result, our whole personality becomes twisted. We end up confused, wounded, lonely, and heartbroken.

The profound simplicity and beauty of marriage is trampled in the mud when we pursue sexual pleasure on its own. The result is broken lives, cynicism, despair, and death. Sex is for life, but to prevent that life we use artificial gadgets, chemicals, and pills — and if that fails, we use more chemicals and finally sharp tools to tear that innocent life from the womb.

Healing Example

A girl in her twenties knocked on my door one afternoon. Sharon's face was a mask of pain and anguish. She came in and told me her story. She was experiencing searing stomach pains. Constant cramp-like pain rippled through her abdomen, and the doctors were baffled. Pain killers didn't touch the pain. She had lost her job because of taking too many days off work. At times, she was doubled over into a fetal position because of the acute shooting pains. I asked her to describe the pain. She said, "It feels like someone is tearing out my insides."

People often describe the real problem in symbolic language, so I asked Sharon about the relationships in her life. The whole story came out of her love affair with an older married man. She became pregnant. Her father kicked her out of the house. Her lover and her father pressured her to have a late-term abortion. When she became sick and depressed, her boyfriend went back to his wife.

I asked some women to help comfort Sharon, and we had a Healing Mass for her. We recognized the life of the innocent victim and gave the child to God. We asked for Sharon's healing and forgiveness. When I saw her the next week, I hardly recognized her. The mask of pain was gone. The stomach pains had totally ceased. Within a few months, she had met a decent young man of her own age, and it was my great joy to officiate at Sharon's wedding a year later.

Pray for Healing

As you meditate on the wedding at Cana, can you see the quiet presence of Jesus and Mary there in the background? They don't take center stage. Their presence is behind the love that is being celebrated. Like the miraculous wine, Jesus and Mary provide a new and joyful energy source for the love of marriage. The wine flowing into and through the whole celebration, through the people at the celebration, is a symbol of how God's grace should flow through our lives, purifying the sexual instinct, driving it toward a pure and wholesome expression, and bringing us to share in God's creation of new life. Behind the wine and the source of the wine is the life-giving power of Jesus Christ. It is his love that should empower our love. It is his power of creation that should flow through our pro-creative potential. Like wine — which fills, warms, and makes joyful — it is Christ's quiet and confident presence that should empower and fill our own attempts at human love.

Where is your life when it comes to marriage, love, and sexuality? Are you married? What is the state of your marriage? Is it fully open to life? Is it fully open to God's grace, power, and love? Are you unmarried? Is your sexual life bogged down in pointless fantasy, pornography, or selfish pleasure? Are you involved in a relationship that is empty, destructive, and going nowhere? Are you desperately seeking in a human relationship that love which only God can give?

What is your past like? Are there relationships from the past that were destructive? Did you use another person and discard them like a piece of trash? Did you prevent or destroy the life that comes from sexual relations through artificial and intentional means? Most of us do these things without meaning to harm anyone. We mean well, but the hurt still happens.

Imagine Jesus and Mary walking into that wedding feast. They are walking into this area of your life right now. Can you feel the power of their purity? Can you feel the forgiving power of Christ's love? Can you feel the compassion and understanding he has for you? Can you feel Mary's maternal love and concern for you? She is a virgin and a mother. He is the master healer. They understand all of your longings for love. They know your powerful instincts, and they understand all the mistakes you have made. Like the noisy, busy wedding feast, your own emotions in the area of love and sexuality are a mixture of joy, fear, ecstasy, and confusion. You want to give love, but you are desperate to be loved.

Let it all go. Allow the unconditional love of God the Father to be expressed to you through the sacrifice of Christ and the loving concern of his mother and yours. Through the beauty of marriage, God wants to heal every aspect of distorted sexuality. The powerful purity of Mary will help to straighten out what is crooked. Put the sins from your past under the mercy of God. Imagine the wine at the wedding feast being poured out. The wine is also a symbol of Christ's blood being shed for you. The huge jars are full and overflowing with his forgiveness. All you need to do is open your heart and accept.

If this process brings past sins to mind, you should take them to confession. Remember that you should bring the sins you have committed, but you may also bring the sins of which you are a victim. Pray for the people who hurt you and ask for God's healing, and for them to be forgiven too. As Jesus did something new and unexpected in providing the wine at the wedding feast, and as you come to know his forgiveness, look for him to do something new and wonderful in your life of love.

❖

Thank God for This Gift

Dear heavenly Father, thank you for the gift of love and sexuality. Through the death of your Son, Jesus Christ, forgive all my distorted and misguided attempts at finding love. Through the prayers of Mary, ever-Virgin, may I be guided into a pure, fruitful, and wonderful love. Like new wine, may this love fill my life and bring me to the divine fullness of love that only you can give. This I pray through Christ, my bridegroom and the source of all love. Amen.

PREACHING THE KINGDOM
The Prime of Life

Now after John was arrested, Jesus came into Galilee, preaching the gospel of God, and saying, "The time is fulfilled, and the kingdom of God is at hand; repent, and believe in the gospel."

MARK 1:14-15

Can you picture Jesus in the prime of his ministry? Crowds are gathering, and his fame is growing. The people are demanding. This person wants to be healed, that person has questions, and another person simply wants his attention. At the same time, storm clouds are gathering. His success brings critics. Other men are jealous, suspicious, and negative. In the midst of his growing fame, and all the pressures of working at his optimum, Jesus continually takes time to pray. Can you see him distance himself from the crowds?

He's taking a time-out. He's slipping away to be alone with God. Only through his prayer/work balance can he continue to preach and minister, because he knows that only through constant contact with his Father will he keep strong, stay focused, and find the energy to pursue his mission to the end.

Think It Through

There are few things more exciting than seeing men and women working at their optimum performance, doing what they do best. Whether it is an athlete, a musician, a mother, a father, a businessman, a nurse or a doctor — when someone is doing well what he or she loves, you can glimpse real human potential at its zenith. As we enter into the prime of life, we should be at the place where the years of preparation, training, and apprenticeship come to fulfillment. Whatever vocation we have discovered in earlier life has now matured, and we enter into our prime. We are firing on all cylinders. We are living life to the full: giving and creating and producing an abundance from all that we have worked on up to that point.

Unfortunately, life is not always like that. Many of us are disappointed by the midpoint in our lives. Perhaps we had the wrong expectations to start with, or we persevered for a long time in a dead-end job. Maybe we never discovered our true vocation, and believe it is too late. Maybe all the great things we wanted for ourselves and our families have not materialized and we taste only the bitterness of failure. At this stage in life, it is easy to give in to despair. Sometimes, instead of the bitterness of despair, we set off on some ill-fated adventure to reclaim our lost youth, or create a fantasy life for ourselves.

What we can't see in the midst of disappointment and a sense of failure is that even "successful" people experience the same sense of loss at the midpoint of life. If a person has never developed his spiritual life, then the loss he feels at midlife is a hunger for the spiritual. If a man has spent his whole life making money to support his family, and a woman has spent her whole life looking after her husband and family, when the children have gone they can feel empty, and their life seems pointless. If, however, they have always looked beyond their career, their family, and their own ambitions, and looked to God, then they will never be disappointed.

Healing Example

Susan was married to Tom. They had four beautiful children and had adopted a fifth child from a Romanian orphanage. Tom had a good job and supported the family well. He loved the children and was devoted to Susan. Then one day everything went wrong. Susan started on a fitness craze that took her away from the home more and more. She began a love affair with another married man and announced that she was leaving Tom. Susan moved out with the children and moved in with her new man.

Tom was devastated. The two teenage daughters were confused, angry, and thrown into rebellion and insecurity through their mother's selfish action. Friends got involved and tried to reason with Susan, but her mind was made up. She insisted on following the path she had set on. Eventually, her new man went back to his wife and family. Tom tried to support them from a distance, but Susan wouldn't have him back. The older daughters moved into small apartments. One developed an eating disorder. Another became pregnant, had an abortion, then became depressed and began abusing drugs. One horrible night, at the age of twenty, she was found dead in her small apartment from a violent reaction to the drugs she had been taking.

Susan's negative reaction to her situation in midlife caused endless heartache and destruction. Like the rest of her friends, there was nothing I could do for Susan except watch the sad story unfold.

Pray for Healing

The only thing that can take us through the difficult middle stages of life is a growing prayer life. Can you see Jesus, in the midst of his ministry, taking time to pray? Can you sense the power, the insights, and the clear direction he receives from the

Father through prayer? Jesus is totally dependent on his relationship with the Father in heaven. Prayer is his meat and drink. Prayer is his life's breath. As you meditate on Jesus in the midst of his preaching ministry, sense the power within his preaching. It comes from prayer. Why does Jesus preach the need for repentance? Because repentance is the constant realization that we need God, and that we need to pray. Why does Jesus constantly invite us to enter the kingdom? Because the kingdom of God is life with God in prayer.

Where is your life in this process? Are you at the beginning of your adult life? If so, do not neglect prayer. Learning to pray is the work of a lifetime. Start early. Are you in the middle stage of life now? Are you disappointed? Are you tempted to become resentful, jealous of others, and bitter about what you have not accomplished? Turn to prayer. It will help you to see things from a new perspective. Are you tempted to run away, to embark on some pointless adventure, or to try to recreate your youth in a way that would damage yourself and others? It is God you are seeking, not youth. Turn to prayer. Have you passed through this stage having done things you regret? Maybe you have reached middle age and have been active in your prime, but all it has brought you is material wealth, pride, and arrogance. Turn to prayer. Prayer will correct you.

See and hear Jesus Christ preaching the kingdom, and bring him into the middle of your life. Allow his strength, wisdom, and confidence to fill your heart and mind. His fame did not affect him. He was not distracted by worldly standards of "success." He knew his vocation and followed the call. Claim his strength of purpose, his self-knowledge, and his total trust in the Father's goodness. Do you still not know your vocation in middle life? Allow Christ to give you a vocation before it is too late. Imagine his energy, compassion, and outgoing love to fill your life with a new zeal, a new power, and a deep new love for others. Are you filled with fear and despair at this stage of life? See how Jesus turns to prayer, and let him teach you to pray in the power of the Holy Spirit.

If you have gone through this stage of life and done things you regret that harmed yourself and others, take it to confession. It is never too late to receive forgiveness and healing, and to start again.

Thank God for This Gift

Heavenly Father, grant me the gift to see myself as you see me. Help me not to despair at my seeming failure or to be proud of my apparent success. Instead, grant me the power and insight that comes from a deep life of prayer. Help me to repent and enter the kingdom of God, and through the prayers of Mary, ever my loving Mother, may I learn again to be your child. This I ask through Christ my Lord. Amen.

TRANSFIGURATION
The Face of Christ

[Jesus] took with him Peter and John and James, and went up on the mountain to pray. And as he was praying, the appearance of his countenance was altered, and his raiment became dazzling white. And behold, two men talked with him, Moses and Elijah, who appeared in glory and spoke of his exodus, which he was to accomplish at Jerusalem.

LUKE 9:28-31

The three disciples don't know what they're getting into. Jesus takes them to Mount Tabor to pray, and suddenly they see Jesus as he really is. The carpenter's son from Nazareth is transfigured, and he appears in radiant glory with Moses and Elijah from the Old Testament. For a moment, they not only see Jesus as he really is, but they also see everything else in the light of his presence. They see the essence of Jesus' whole being, and by that vision they feel more fully the sinful condition at the core of their being, and they respond the only way they can: with worship.

Think It Through

Prayer changes the way we look at the whole world. At the heart of prayer is the silence in which we contemplate the face of Christ. This prayer beyond words takes us into the mystery of Christ. As we do this, we experience the Christ-life at the depth of our being — and as he was transfigured on Mount

Tabor, his presence transfigures us. Slowly, as we contemplate the face of Christ, we are transformed into his likeness. We become like the thing we worship. So as we use the Rosary to meditate on the pattern of Christ's life, our life is increasingly conformed to the pattern of his life. All Christians are called to the contemplative life. We may not have the time to spend in adoration and contemplation that monks and nuns do, but at the heart of our prayer life must be silent time simply spent in the presence of Christ.

How many of us have learned to spend time in silence with Christ? Instead, we would do almost anything else but spend time in silence with Christ. Christ is total and utter reality — so if we lose touch with him, we lose touch with reality. We get a distorted vision of the world. We fall for illusions. We lose the right priorities and start drifting through life like a ship without a rudder. Because we will not spend time alone with Christ, our vision becomes clouded. We cannot see ourselves, our families, and our world clearly. Instead of allowing the radiance of the transfigured Christ to bring us clarity of vision and simplicity of soul, we become confused and stumble through life meaning well, but constantly getting it wrong, causing ourselves and others yet more pain, grief, anguish, and sorrow.

If we have not seen Christ as he really is, then it is impossible to see anything else as it really is. Most of all, if we haven't seen Christ as he really is, we can't see ourselves as we really are. Like the sun, Christ is the light by which we see all things. Without that light, we are lost in the darkness — even if we think we've got all the answers.

Healing Example

I once met Mother Teresa of Calcutta. I was visiting India with a friend and we decided to take a collection to the Missionaries of Charity. When we arrived at the famous mother-house in Calcutta, we saw a little sign on the door that read "Mother is in." The cheerful nun at the reception table asked us if we would like to meet Mother Teresa. We were thrilled at the opportunity to chat with Mother Teresa for five minutes. She asked if we had come to work, and was disappointed to learn that we had only brought a check.

It was wonderful to visit with Mother Teresa, but it was even more wonderful to spend just a moment with her in the simple chapel. As she knelt before the Blessed Sacrament, the atmosphere of love and power was almost tangible. At that moment, the sheer reality — hard, beautiful, radiant reality — of Mother Teresa's life and ministry came rolling across me like a waterfall.

Pray for Healing

The healing love of Christ at this stage of the Rosary is touching us at the deepest level — the level of our soul beyond words. We are all wounded and needy at this level of our lives, but in a way that we can scarcely express. The only way to minister to this depth of our heart, which is beyond language, is through prayer without language. One of the best ways to experience the healing love of Christ at the depth of our soul is by getting to know him through the silent contemplation of his glory.

Can you imagine what it must have been like with the disciples at the transfiguration of Jesus into glory? At that moment, life was not less real, but more real. At that moment, every blade of grass, every leaf on every tree, and every cloud in the sky must have felt like it had another color or dimension to it. Can you sense the sheer power and reality of that moment?

That clear and radiant light penetrates to the core of our being. It reveals both the depth of our emptiness without

Christ and the amazing fullness of his love for us. What have you seen more clearly about yourself as a result of contemplating the face of Christ? Have you seen some faults? Have you seen your foolish pride? Have you seen how empty you are without Christ? On the other hand, have you also seen how much Christ loves you? Have you sensed how much his radiant light burns from his Sacred Heart of love for you? Have you seen that his light and love transform all your weaknesses into his strength? Have you seen and felt how overwhelmingly he loves you?

If the light of the transfigured Christ has revealed something to your very core condition, you may not be able to put it into words. If what you've seen is negative, bring it to God in confession. Simply say, "I confess my emptiness without Christ and ask for his light to fill me and heal me at the deepest level of my being." At the very heart of your existence — at the very heart of who you are — receive God's unconditional love and power. You are his child. He made you for his own. Know that underneath you are the everlasting arms.

Thank God for This Gift

Heavenly Father, I thank you that your Son, Jesus Christ, was born of the Virgin Mary and became man. Take me deeper into the light of Christ, and by that light may I see myself and all things clearly. As I see all things in the light of Christ, help me to love all things as he loves them. This I ask in the name of Jesus, my radiant Master and Lord. Amen.

INSTITUTION OF THE EUCHARIST
Relationship With the Church

"I am the living bread which came down from heaven; if any one eats of this bread, he will live for ever; and the bread which I shall give for the life of the world is my flesh."

"I came that they may have life, and have it abundantly."

JOHN 6:51; 10:10

J esus is gathered with his closest friends for their final meal together. As they celebrate the Passover, they are united with one another and with him. Can you sense the fellowship they share around the table? Can you imagine the small room, the smell of the smoky oil lamps, and the soft glow of the flames? At this ritual meal, they are bringing the action of the Passover into the present moment and becoming one with God's saving and healing work in the world. In ways far more profound than they can presently understand, they are becoming one with the body of Christ, and joining themselves with God's one, full, final sacrifice.

Think It Through

We are at our best when we are giving ourselves in sacrifice. This is the height of the human experience. We may give ourselves in pursuit of excellence in sports, music, academics, or the arts. We may lay down our lives in a caring profession, in spiritual service, in prayer, or in the self-giving within marriage and family life. In whatever way we lay down our lives, it is in this laying down of our lives that we find heroes. The word "hero" means "one who makes a sacrifice," and this sacrificial principle runs like a scarlet thread through all of our human existence. It is the summit of what it means to be human.

Unfortunately, we often learn this lesson too late in life. It is our nature *not* to lay down our lives in willing sacrifice, but to assert ourselves in selfishness, pleasure, pride, and willfulness. When we live this way, sadness, hurt, pain, and grief are the result. We can never have true friendships if we are self-seeking. Our marriages will never succeed if we are selfish. Even our careers falter through selfishness, aggression, and pride. Our refusal to lay down our lives in sacrifice to God and to others is at the root of most of our unhappiness, ill health, stress, anxiety, and fear. It is not simply that we ourselves are to blame for the lack of self-sacrifice, but that we are caught up in a network of selfish people. All of the world's ills have the same root: self-centeredness. Most of the world's ills have the same cure: self-sacrifice.

Self-sacrifice leads us to dynamic, good relationships with others. Self-centeredness leads to isolation, loneliness, and despair. In the Eucharist, the self-sacrifice of Christ leads to the perfect communion. It leads to communion with him, communion with one another, communion with God, and communion with the whole created order. This happens as we submit ourselves to the sacred mystery that is the Mass.

Healing Example

I wish I had space to tell all the stories of healing and reconciliation that have happened through the miracle of the Mass. I have seen families converted, broken marriages restored, and deep wounds from the past healed. I have seen the emotionally and spiritually dead restored to life in Christ, the sick healed, and demons cast out. I have known inner peace restored, bitterness of heart replaced with sweetness and hope, a cold faith rekindled, and the burden of guilt totally lifted. Day by day I have seen spiritual lives empowered, minds blinded by sin opened to the light of Christ, enemies reconciled, and peace established in broken lives.

Pray for Healing

The healing love of Christ was given to us for all time as he instituted the Eucharist. At that point, his own self-sacrifice was enshrined for all time as a permanent memorial. Can you put yourself into that place and time? At that moment, Jesus Christ's self-giving charged each one present with the supernatural power of his healing love.

Consider your own life. Has it been broken by selfishness? Have your hopes and dreams been shattered by the selfishness of others? Has your selfishness broken the lives of other people? Do you suffer from stress, anxiety, and a broken heart because of the selfish aggression of other people? Are your illnesses due to the fact that you bear bitterness and an unforgiving spirit toward those who have wounded you? This, too, is a form of selfishness. The answer is to meditate on what Jesus Christ gave us as he instituted the Eucharist. At that point, he revealed himself as the one whose body would be broken, and whose love would be poured out. Can you cling to his self-sacrifice, and next time you go to Mass receive his self-sacrifice? Can you open your heart and receive his forgiveness and healing? Only by doing this will you have the power and grace to live a life of forgiveness and self-sacrifice.

When you receive Communion at Mass, you receive the saving sacrifice of Christ on the cross. Through the sacrifice of the Mass, that one, full, final sacrifice is made real and present for your forgiveness and healing. As you meditate on this mystery in the Rosary, allow the reality of what Christ has done for you to penetrate every part of your body, mind, and spirit. Allow the Holy Spirit to bring to mind any selfish thought, word, or action that has separated you from God and from others. Next time you go to confession, bring these things for forgiveness and ask for the spirit of self-giving instead of self-centeredness. God will give you a desire to serve others — and as you do, the hurt and pain that has resulted from the selfishness you have suffered will eventually be healed.

Thank God for This Gift

Father in heaven, I give you thanks and praise for the sacrifice of your Son, Jesus Christ, on the cross of Calvary. I repent of my selfishness and sin. I have caused suffering in others, and have suffered because of the selfishness of others. Lift from me the burden of my selfish desire and replace it with the spirit of sacrifice and love that comes from Jesus Christ. This I pray with Mary, whose own heart was pierced in the agony of self-giving. As I learn to take up my cross and follow Christ, grant me the healing and forgiveness that is your will for me. Amen.

III

The Sorrowful
Mysteries

AGONY IN THE GARDEN
Facing Despair

And he came out, and went, as was his custom, to the Mount of Olives; and the disciples followed him. And when he came to the place he said to them, "Pray that you may not enter into temptation." And he withdrew from them about a stone's throw, and knelt down and prayed, "Father, if you are willing, remove this chalice from me; nevertheless not my will, but yours, be done."

LUKE 22:39-42

On his knees, Jesus faces the heart of darkness. In the Garden of Gethsemane, everything seems lost. He knows the only way forward is torture and death, but pleads for there to be some other way. More than the fear of physical pain and the agony of death, Jesus faces the pain of misunderstanding, loneliness, and betrayal — and beyond this, the devil's wish to make him feel worthless and so give in to despair. Jesus senses that all his friends will turn away. His enemies will triumph. All the good he has tried to do seems wasted. All the truth he has tried to live is spat upon. All the love he has tried to give has been rejected, and he faces torture and death from the very ones he has tried to help.

Think It Through

All of us mean well. We want what is good for ourselves, our families, and our friends. Most of us want to help others, and to live in loving relationships that lead to prosperity, happiness, and an abundant life. When we give to others, it is natural that we long to be appreciated, loved, and honored for all that we've done. It is natural to want our gifts, abilities, and hard work to be recognized and applauded. Our desire to be appreciated is part of our deeper desire to be loved totally and unconditionally.

Unfortunately, life doesn't always work out that way. Instead of appreciation, we're taken for granted. Instead of honor, we're ignored. Employers drive us hard so they can make as much profit as possible. Family members take us for granted and blame us for their own mistakes. People we try to help throw it back in our faces or are totally oblivious of our efforts for them. Those in authority don't seem to know we exist — and if we try to impress them with our gifts, hard work, and good ideas, they are suspicious. They imagine we have an "agenda" and marginalize us. Are we surprised this happens to us when we have been so unappreciative of others? When our own life is driven by our ache to be loved and honored and appreciated, are we surprised that other people are totally self-absorbed as well?

In the Sorrowful Mysteries, we come closest to our need for deep inner healing. These mysteries bring us to the awareness of our needs that are deeper than all words. At the heart of the darkness in the Garden of Gethsemane is the utter loneliness and alienation that each of us experiences. Sometimes, in the depths of depression or loneliness, we feel it acutely. More often it surfaces as a nagging hunger for companionship, approval, affection, and human love. However it appears, this is the agony of Gethsemane. At the heart of this lack of appreciation, rejection, and betrayal in our human relationships is our alienation from God — the source of Love itself.

Healing Example

Bob was a successful businessman with a beautiful family. He attended church and was a respectable and popular man in his mid-forties. Then he asked whether his faith was real, and whether it made any difference in his life. That's when things started to unravel. He met a counselor who helped him to meet Jesus Christ for the first time. His life was dismantled, as all his facades fell away. For the first time, he saw how worthless he felt. The abuse he suffered as a child came flooding back, and with it the deep feelings that he was worthless, abandoned, totally unloved, repugnant, and rejected.

At the heart of his darkness, Bob met Jesus, the despised and rejected one — and in a way too deep to describe, he realized that in Jesus Christ he was totally loved and accepted. As he worked through the painful memories, Jesus was there every step of the way. The healing Bob went through took a long time. It was painful, and he required enormous courage, but through the sorrowful mystery of his own life Bob met Jesus Christ — who brings healing, peace, and abundant life.

Pray for Healing

Can you visualize Jesus in the Garden of Gethsemane? He senses that almost all his friends will forsake him. He senses that the darkness will be even deeper than that, and that he will even feel abandoned by God the Father. In this moment, Jesus Christ faces the alienation and loneliness that each of us feels individually, and which the whole human race suffers under. In loneliness, he accepts the loneliness. In fear, he accepts the fear. In the loneliness, he is tempted to despair, to give up, to lose his faith, and to abandon God. Still, he stays the course and turns to give his life as his betrayer comes.

Have you felt abandoned, unloved, and unappreciated? Have colleagues, friends, and lovers let you down? Have parents disappointed you, or have siblings cast you aside? Have your relationships gone wrong, and have you been left without the love and acceptance you long for? Have you always loved and appreciated others as much as you should have? Have you disappointed others? Have you hurt, rejected, or betrayed anyone?

Take all these memories into the Garden of Gethsemane with Jesus Christ. He will take and heal the twisted or distorted parts of your pain, but he also asks you to bear the pain. The real mystery of healing is that we are healed most deeply when we start to share in the passion of Christ. As you meditate on the agony in the garden, allow Christ to heal the pain of your rejection and loneliness, but see if you can also bear the suffering with him, and begin to see how, in accepting the sorrow, his power can help you transform it.

Thank God for This Gift

Heavenly Father, my heart is restless and alone without you. Heal the pain of my human loneliness through knowledge of your unconditional love, but also help me to bear the loneliness of the human race within my own sense of being alone in the world. Through Christ the Lord. Amen.

SCOURGING
Facing Pain

Then he released for them Barabbas, and having scourged Jesus, delivered him to be crucified.

The scourges that the Romans used were strips of leather with sharp bits of metal or broken pottery tied onto them. They ripped into the flesh and tore strips off the victim's back. Jesus is sent out to be flogged, not as a punishment, but to appease the crowd. He is innocent of any wrongdoing, but he suffers severe physical torture. He takes not only the physical pain, but the mental and emotional anguish of being punished for something he never did.

It is easy to say that we are healed through his suffering, and redeemed by his passion. It is much harder to enter the mystery and experience what this means. As you meditate on his sorrowful mysteries, allow the Holy Spirit to take you into an understanding that is beyond words.

Think it Through

Physical pain will come to most of us at some time in our lives. If that pain is the result of something we've done wrong, we might be able to see the reasons and make sense of the pain. If we suffer physical pain as the result of someone else's wrong actions, we can also see where their pain comes from and begin to understand and make sense of it. If the physical pain is the result of old age, an accident, or an injury, it also has some reason and we can learn to accept the pain.

The problem comes when we are hit with physical suffering that seems absurd. Why do people get cancer? Why do strange diseases hit out of nowhere? Why are we born with physical disabilities, diseases, or crippling illnesses? If we're not the ones suffering, we share the pain of our loved ones who are caught in the web of illness and pain, or we sympathize with victims of natural disaster, famine, and plague. We can honestly say we didn't do anything to deserve these physical sorrows. In one sense, we're innocent victims. That's why the suffering is more than physical pain — because we can't make sense of it. It seems absurd and evil.

As we meditate on Jesus enduring the cruel scourging, we are taken into the heart of evil. Evil seeks innocent victims. That is why it is so evil. If only wicked people suffered, we wouldn't consider suffering to be evil at all. Instead, the wicked seem to get away with it and ordinary good people are hit with terrible suffering. There seems to be no justice. There seems to be no reason except that a horrible force in the world not only inflicts pain and suffering but also chooses innocent victims.

Healing Example

Sister Clare is a nun. She has been a contemplative for more than fifty years, and for most of that time she has been blind. For a time, the doctors were able to restore her sight, but then the shadows descended and she was left in darkness again. Now, as an old woman, she has become a hermit. She is alone in the woods with her God and with her suffering. In addition to the blindness, Sister Clare has curvature of the spine and is in constant pain. I have never heard her complain. Instead, she greets me with a radiant smile, and when I ask about the pain she says: "Oh, it's not so bad!" When I ask about her eyesight, she says: "You know, I can't bear to see very much. It is all so real — and besides, because I am blind I can see so much more that other people can't see!"

Sister Clare doesn't deserve her pain. On the contrary, she deserves great bliss and happiness. But she hasn't asked for physical healing. Instead, she is able to enter into the passion of Christ and experience with him the mysterious redemption that comes with sacrifice.

Pray for Healing

Can you glimpse what is going on as Jesus is scourged? Can you sense that something far greater than we can imagine is taking place within his terrible torture? The pain is real. The torture is excruciating, the flesh screams out in agony, but within that innocent suffering a cosmic transaction is taking place. This transaction is the most mysterious and marvelous. It is beyond all words, and it can only be experienced with an inner knowing.

Now reflect on the suffering and pain you have experienced. Did it seem pointless? Maybe there was a reason beyond human reason. Does it seem absurd? Maybe God is doing things through that suffering that we cannot see. If you are in the midst of pain at this time, give it to Jesus as he is scourged. Ask that your pain might be joined with his, and ask for that pain to be used as his was used.

Have you ever caused pain or suffering to another innocent person? Through loss of your temper, violence, or unkindness, have you inflicted pain? In Jesus' scourging, you can see how the pain hurts not just the body but also the emotions and heart of the innocent victim. If something you have done has caused pain, bring it to confession and allow Christ's forgiveness and healing to transform your memories.

❖

Thank God for This Gift

Heavenly Father, by the scourging of your Son, Jesus Christ, help me to understand the deeper mystery of suffering. Take my poor suffering and pain and let it be identified with his. Heal me from the bitterness and lack of faith that come with pain, and help me to know that in your eternal plan there is a deeper beauty and truth that I cannot always see. This I pray through Christ our Lord. Amen.

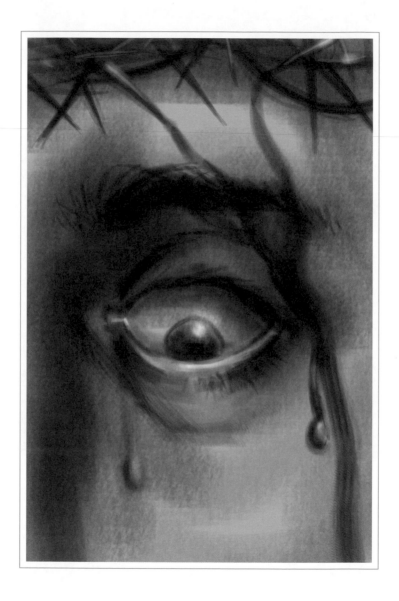

CROWN OF THORNS
Facing Humiliation

*And they stripped him and put a scarlet robe upon him, and plaiting
a crown of thorns they put it on his head, and put a reed in his right
hand. And kneeling before him they mocked him, saying, "Hail, King
of the Jews!" And they spat upon him, and took the reed and struck him
on the head. And when they had mocked him, they stripped him of the
robe, and put his own clothes on him, and led him away to crucify him.*
MATTHEW 27:28-31

They pull Jesus up from the terrible scourging and proceed
to mock him as the King of the Jews. The purple cloak
they hang about him is the color the emperor wears. They
weave a crown of thorns and give him a broken stick for a
scepter. Pushing him to and fro, the soldiers mock and humil-
iate the one who is their Lord and God. The mock crown and
signs of royalty hurt even more because Jesus knows he is the
Lord of glory, but he also knows that the only way back to that
glory is through the bitter suffering he has to face.

Think It Through

All of us want to be recognized for our accomplishments. All
of us want to be recognized for the good things we have done.
More than that, we want to be acknowledged and affirmed
simply for who we are. Beneath this desire is the need for
unconditional love and acceptance. Likewise, we are at our

best in relationships when we recognize the good work, accomplishments, and intrinsic worth of others. To receive and give proper recognition is a form of gratitude. To give and receive recognition is decent, honorable, and good.

How terrible then, when we receive humiliation instead. This form of humiliation is not the development of a clear and honest vision of ourselves, which is called humility. Instead this humiliation is heartless, unfair, and deliberately cruel. How do we feel when our efforts go unnoticed? How do we feel when our gifts are ignored, and we are sidelined and made to feel insignificant? What is it like when our good ideas are laughed at, our initiatives are rebuffed, and our good works are ignored — and no one notices the sacrifices we've made? It hurts.

What about the humiliation we have dished out to others? We may not have deliberately laughed and scorned other people, but how often have we simply ignored others, pushed them to one side, or failed to see their intrinsic worth? How often have we put others down, gossiped about them, or stepped on their dignity because we were jealous of them?

As we see Jesus crowned with thorns, we are taken to the heart of cruel humiliation. He is the King of glory, the Creator of the universe, and yet he is mocked and ridiculed by ignorant, cruel, and hard-hearted men. Jesus takes the humiliation as he took the scourging — in dignified silence. What can he say in the face of such a senseless onslaught? What can anyone do in the face of such mindless hatred? Jesus not only takes the humiliation, but he also takes our humiliation as well. He absorbs the mockery, the cruelty, and the degradation — and he holds it within himself. As he does this, he absorbs all the cruel mockery that the Evil One has doled out to humanity down the ages, and all the cruel mockery that human beings have doled out to one another down the ages.

Healing Example

Michael is a friend of mine who happens to be a brilliant artist. He has genuine talent bursting from every pore. Throughout most of his life, however, he has carried a heavy burden. When he was a boy, his father told him that everything he touched "turned to s**t." Michael believed his father. Throughout childhood and into adulthood, he believed that his talent was worthless, that he would amount to nothing, and that he was destined for failure. Michael became hypersensitive about his artwork. He took the slightest criticism personally, and he became depressed about his life and his work. He once stopped painting for seven years because of one bad review of an art show. The humiliation Michael suffered at an early age affected him for many years. The humiliation was unfair, cruel, and heartless, and it burned a deep wound in his heart.

The worst thing was that his father's words became a kind of prophecy, and Michael didn't enter into the fullness of his talent and life until he brought that humiliation to the feet of Christ in this third sorrowful mystery. As he meditated on Christ's humiliation, his own senseless humiliation became a sharing in the suffering of Christ. And as this happened, Michael gradually began to unfold and recognize his own God-given talent, and he began to reach his potential as an artist, a husband, a father, and a friend.

Pray for Healing

How have you been humiliated? Have you been unappreciated, unrecognized, and cast to one side? Have family members, friends, and colleagues taken you for granted, mocked your ideas, or laughed at your hopes and dreams? Has someone attacked the very heart of your personality by finding what you most treasure and mocking it? Have you seen your dreams and hopes end in disappointment? Has your bitter disappointment been made worse by the seemingly successful lives of others? Do you feel their success burning in your own wound like a bitter fire?

What about your relationship to others? Have you humiliated, ignored, or mocked anyone? Do you need to ask their forgiveness and take your own hardness of heart to confession?

Much of our humiliation is a lack of real humility. Real humility is a clear and honest appreciation of who we are — warts and all. Humility is not groveling in the gutter, but standing simply in God's presence, with a sharp awareness of the gifts he has given us, as well as our own failures and weaknesses. As you meditate on the humiliation of Jesus as he is mocked and crowned with thorns, bring your own humiliations to him. In his light, ask to see yourself clearly and honestly. Do you see how, in the midst of his humiliations, he looks on you with simple clarity, compassion, and love? He doesn't love you for your accomplishments or your gifts. He loves you simply for who you are. He gazes on you as you might gaze on the ones you love most — with simple, unconditional love.

Thank God for This Gift

Heavenly Father, thank you for creating me. I bring to you all my insecurities, self-doubt, and fear. This world is a cruel, heartless, and selfish place. Help me to know your unconditional love and acceptance — and if I have been mocked or humiliated, I can see it was nothing compared to the humiliation Jesus suffered for me. Take what little I have suffered and make it a share in his sufferings, for my healing and for the forgiveness of those who have harmed me. Amen.

CARRYING THE CROSS
Facing Illness and Suffering

And as they led him away, they seized one Simon of Cyrene, who was coming in from the country, and laid on him the cross, to carry it behind Jesus. And there followed him a great multitude of the people, and of women who bewailed and lamented him. But Jesus turning to them said, "Daughters of Jerusalem, do not weep for me, but weep for yourselves and for your children. For behold, the days are coming when they will say, 'Blessed are the barren, and the wombs that never bore, and the breasts that never nursed!' Then they will begin to say to the mountains, 'Fall on us'; and to the hills, 'Cover us.' For if they do this when the wood is green, what will happen when it is dry?"

Two others also, who were criminals, were led away to be put to death with him.

LUKE 23:26-32

The soldiers pull off Jesus' robe and lash the heavy, rough-hewn crossbeam to his shoulders for the next stage of his torture. (The condemned would carry their own cross through the crowded streets in a final journey of humiliation, anguish, and fear.) As Jesus is pushed and shoved on the way, he falls under the weight, and the cross crushes him to the ground. Fearing that he may pass out or die before he can be crucified, the soldiers force Simon of Cyrene to take up Jesus' cross. The gospel says Simon followed Jesus as he staggered through the crowded narrow streets to the place of execution.

Think It Through

Wouldn't it be wonderful if we could go through life without facing illness, pain, and suffering? We expend so much time, effort, and money to avoid pain. We work hard to keep fit, to have good medical care, to eat well, and to create pain-free lives. Our society encourages us to build a beautiful, comfortable, and painless existence, and we conspire together to marginalize illness, isolate the suffering, and push pain to the edge of our existence. Even when we know that suffering, pain, and illness are on the way, we do everything we can to avoid them. We hope for a painless treatment of our illness and then a quick and merciful death.

This is not very realistic. In fact, all of us will face illness, pain, and suffering one way or another. No matter how much we try to keep fit and eat well, and no matter how good our medical system is, we will face illness and suffering. Whether it is through an accident, disease, or simply old age, the unholy trinity of illness, pain, and suffering will visit us. Even if we ourselves manage to avoid a serious meeting with these three, we will share the anguish of our loved ones going through suffering. And even if our family and friends are spared a terrible ordeal, we still experience the inner anguish of insecurity, depression, loneliness, and fear.

As we see Jesus staggering through the streets with his cross strapped to his shoulders, we are seeing the way to handle illness, pain, and suffering. There is no way around it: these dark companions through life are to be borne with dignity, grace, and courage. It is true that Jesus wants to heal us, but it is also true that he calls us to take up our cross and follow him. There comes a time when we are called to the deeper healing of accepting our illness, pain, and suffering as an opportunity to share in the suffering of Christ, and to share willingly in the cross he bore.

We are also called to share the burden of the cross borne by others. If we are blessed with very little pain, suffering, and illness, then how do we *take up our cross and follow him* (see Mt 16:24, Mk 8:34, Lk 9:23)? We share in the suffering of the world by compassionate care for those who are in the midst of suffering. Are we actively involved in caring for the sick, the dying, the dispossessed, the prisoners, the hungry, and the poor? Inasmuch as we minister to them, we are taking up our cross and following Christ.

Healing Example

My father was a healthy, lively man who loved life. He had hardly been sick a day in his life. In his retirement, he traveled, went on Christian mission trips, skied, played tennis, and swam. He enjoyed his grandchildren, his wife, his family, and his friends.

Then, seemingly out of nowhere, he was struck with liver failure. He started a rapid decline, and then his pastor and members of his church visited him. He confessed his sins and received anointing for healing, and he began to feel better. He continued to fight the disease, but for another two years he went into a slow decline. He looked for a cure and consulted the best doctors. More drugs were prescribed, and he struggled with the side effects of a daily cocktail of drugs. Still he fought for life and believed he would get better. Then the results of another test came through. There was a tumor on the liver. There was nothing else the doctor could do.

When I came to visit him, it was the day Dad had to go into the hospice for the dying. I drove him to his final home and helped him into bed. We talked for a bit about his life and his coming death and he said, "I've tried hard to show people how to live. Now I have one more job . . . to show people how to die."

As a Christian, Dad did just that. He struggled and raged against the horror of illness and pain, but in the end he took up his cross and followed Christ. A few months later he died peacefully, with his work done.

Pray for Healing

Are you struggling with the horrors of illness, pain, and suffering? Are your family and friends facing disease, injury, or death? How do you cope? How does anyone cope? The Christian way is to ask for healing. The Christian way is to fight against the horror of illness, suffering, and death. The Christian way is to affirm life and fight for life. The Christian way is also to accept that illness and suffering will come to us all. When we are ready, the mysterious way of Christ is for us to take up our cross and follow him.

Can you see him as he falls and drops the cross? Are you standing in the crowd? Do the soldiers pick you to bear the cross of Christ instead of Simon of Cyrene? What is your decision?

When we enter illness, pain, and suffering, we are entering into the very heart of the mystery of love. At the heart of the mystery of love is the mystery of sacrifice. Only when we take up the cross of Christ do we really begin to enter into that mystery fully. Only then can we make final sense of the suffering in our lives, the suffering of our loved ones, and the suffering of the whole of the human race. As you meditate on Jesus Christ carrying his cross, hand over to him all the pain, suffering, and illness in your life and in the life of your loved ones. Ask for his healing, and then ask for the grace to carry the cross and to bear the final burden along with him. Can you fathom the mystery that through this transaction your own suffering is being transformed into part of his mysterious redemption? This is where words stop and the pure power of God's love begins.

Thank God for This Gift

Father God, I cannot bear my own sufferings, much less the sufferings of the whole world. Relieve my pain, heal my illness, and lift the burden of my suffering. If this is not your will, then grant me the grace to bear the suffering in the name of Christ. Use it to bring me closer to his love. Put my suffering into his so that as he helps me to bear it, my suffering may be used to complete his sufferings for the redemption of the world. This I plead through Christ my Lord. Amen.

CRUCIFIXION
Facing Death

And when they came to a place called Golgotha (which means the place of a skull), they offered him wine to drink, mingled with gall; but when he tasted it, he would not drink it. And when they had crucified him, they divided his garments among them by casting lots; then they sat down and kept watch over him there. And over his head they put the charge against him, which read, "This is Jesus the King of the Jews." Then two robbers were crucified with him, one on the right and one on the left. And those who passed by derided him, wagging their heads and saying, "You who would destroy the temple and build it in three days, save yourself! If you are the Son of God, come down from the cross." So also the chief priests, with the scribes and elders, mocked him, saying, "He saved others; he cannot save himself. He is the King of Israel; let him come down now from the cross, and we will believe in him. He trusts in God; let God deliver him now, if he desires him; for he said, 'I am the Son of God.'" And the robbers who were crucified with him also reviled him in the same way.

Now from the sixth hour there was darkness over all the land until the ninth hour. And about the ninth hour Jesus cried with a loud voice, "Eli, Eli, lama sabach-thani?" that is, "My God, my God, why have you forsaken me?" And some of the bystanders hearing it said, "This man is calling Elijah." And one of them at once ran and took a sponge, filled it with vinegar, and put it on a reed, and gave it to him to drink. But the others said, "Wait, let us see whether Elijah will come to save him." And Jesus cried again with a loud voice and yielded up his spirit.

MATTHEW 27:33-50

Jesus finally arrives at Golgotha — the place of the skull, the place of death. Crucifixion is the worst form of torture and death because the victim remains suspended in agony for hours, often for days. As Jesus is nailed to the cross and hung up to die, he is abandoned by all but his mother, the apostle John, and a few women disciples. Hanging naked, for the world to see, Jesus faces the final enemy in physical agony. His inner torment is even greater. He feels that his Father has abandoned him as well, and he is tempted to despair and even the loss of faith. Still, in the midst of his anguish, he is able to plead for forgiveness for his tormentors, and to share his love and forgiveness with one who is crucified with him. Finally, it is finished, and his lifeless body hangs above a lonely world, a sign of the vulnerable power of God to all who killed him.

Think It Through

Death stalks us in every moment of life. Happily, we go through most days not thinking of death. Our society conspires together with us to put death out of our minds. Entertainment, work, family life, and constant activity help distract us from death. Good food, good health care, and a discreet way of dealing with death help to shield us from the grim reality of the grim reaper. The crucifix helps to correct this shallow obsession with a superficially happy life.

Whenever we see a crucifix, we should be reminded that death comes to us all. Sooner or later we will face the final lonely journey to the realm of the dead. In earlier ages, when death was more of a daily possibility, Christians were more aware of the need to prepare for death. We would do well to keep death daily before our eyes. We do this not because we are morbid or grim-faced, but because it focuses our lives and helps us to establish the right priorities. Life is a preparation for death, and the Christian should view every day as an opportunity to prepare for eternity.

As we see Jesus lying on his cross and being nailed down, then hung up to die, we are brought face-to-face with our own death one day. We're brought face-to-face with the reality of our sin, and the fact that death is only in the world because of sin. As Jesus dies, he really does die for the whole world. He takes on the sin that causes death. He battles with Satan, who loves death. He embraces the darkness of death for the whole of humanity. As we consider our own sin and our own unavoidable death, we can only ask for his mercy and humbly put our death into his death so that we might also share in his new life.

Healing Example

When I was living in London, I was invited, along with some other Christian leaders, to a preview of Mel Gibson's film *The Passion of the Christ*. It was rumored that Gibson might be present to ask for our comments and reactions. Sure enough, after the film a quiet, unassuming man took the stage as the lights came up. Gibson asked for our views and took notes for the final editing of the film. We also had the chance to ask the famous actor and director about his intentions.

He shared his own witness, of how he was brought up as a Catholic and then went his own way. He fell into the big-time temptations of Hollywood, wealth, and fame. Then he went on retreat and came face-to-face with himself through a deep reflection on the mystery of the Crucifixion. He realized that his own sin and death were locked into the death of Jesus Christ. Then he told us that the actor in the close-up shot of a soldier's hands picking up the hammer and spikes and nailing Jesus' hands to the cross was him, and that it was his hands crucifying the Lord.

For Mel Gibson, making *The Passion of the Christ* was a profound meditation on the death of Jesus. His spiritual life was renewed as he knew his sins were forgiven, and his career and priorities in life were straightened out. There might be future failures, but he knew the direction of his life was settled for good.

Pray for Healing

What is your attitude toward your eventual death? It could happen at any time. Are you prepared? Have you accepted in your heart what you accept in your head — that Jesus Christ died on the cross to save you from eternal death? This is what the gospel is all about. It is simple. Jesus died for you. Jesus died for me. Like love, this is a mystery that cannot be fully explained. It can only be accepted or rejected. The way to accept this gift is to realize that it was your hands that helped nail Christ to the cross. It was your sin that brought him to that place. It was your fear, pride, jealousy, and hatred that helped to crucify him, and it was to wash this sin away that he took it to the cross and nailed it there to pay the price.

As you meditate on the mystery of the cross, do not bother to try to understand. Simply try to know in your heart, and to accept at the deepest level of your being, that Christ died for you.

The mystery of love expressed in the death of Christ goes to the very foundations of our personality. There at the depths, each one of us has an aching need to be loved totally and unconditionally. At the very heart of us we all long for a friend who loves us so much that he would lay down his life for us. The aching need for this kind of love, and the longing desire for this love, are what cause us to seek love in so many false ways that eventually lead to greed, lust, addictions, and eventually to loneliness, fear, anxiety, and despair. The remedy for all these ills is to know the love of Christ on the cross and to yield that deepest, darkest corner of our lives to him.

At the cross, our greatest need meets his greatest gift. Stop, and let him minister that love to you.

❖

Thank God for This Gift

Heavenly Father, I offer simple thanks and praise for the wonder of Christ's love for me. I am sorry for my lack of love, fear, and selfish seeking for love in all the wrong places. I accept that Jesus Christ died for me, and I ask for the power of his loving death to fill the empty space in my heart with his never-ending forgiveness, light, and peace. Amen.

IV

The Glorious
Mysteries

RESURRECTION
Claiming Christ's Victory

Now after the sabbath, toward the dawn of the first day of the week, Mary Magdalene and the other Mary went to see the tomb. And behold, there was a great earthquake; for an angel of the Lord descended from heaven and came and rolled back the stone, and sat upon it. His appearance was like lightning, and his clothing white as snow. And for fear of him the guards trembled and became like dead men. But the angel said to the women, "Do not be afraid; for I know that you seek Jesus who was crucified. He is not here; for he has risen, as he said. Come, see the place where he lay."

MATTHEW 28:1-6

Jesus couldn't stay dead. How can you kill Life itself? On the third day his glory was manifested as he rose from the dead. His resurrection was the final victory over evil. As he burst from the tomb on Easter morning, he trampled on suffering, pain, illness, and death once and for all. His victory was like a seed being planted in the history of the world. Once he rose from the dead, he gave the power to all who follow him to also claim the victory over the world, the flesh, and the devil.

Think It Through

Wouldn't it be wonderful if we could claim the victory over sin and death? Wouldn't you like to banish temptation, sin, suffering, doubt, and fear forever? What would it be like if you could overcome sin and live in the glorious power of the Resurrection? If we could do this, we would be saints. We would reach our full potential and be all that God created us to be.

To get there, however, is the work of a lifetime. Instead of the victory of Christ's resurrection, we fall back into the negativity of sin. Each Sunday, as we go to Mass, we celebrate the Resurrection, but too often we miss the power of that celebration and drift back into selfishness, greed, lust, violence, and despair. This should not cause us to give up, however. The Christian life is a long, hard journey, and to come to our final victory we need patience, perseverance, and a constant turning away from our sin and toward the victory that Christ has won for us.

As we meditate on the Resurrection, we are likely to praise God for Christ's victory over sin, but we are also likely to see how far short we are from fully realizing his resurrection power in our lives. It is wonderful to contemplate Christ's glorious victory, but it is not so wonderful to be reminded of our own repeated failures. We want to run in the path of Christian perfection and total victory, but all we seem to do is stumble and fall.

Healing Example

Martin had committed his life to Christ as a teenager at a high school retreat. He wanted to live the Christian life, but in his teenage years he started to use pornography. He had girlfriends, but he was also attracted to other guys. In college, he had a string of short-lived sexual encounters with other men. Whenever this happened, he went to confession and tried again to follow Christ.

Eventually, Martin got married. He loved his wife and they had three beautiful children. When he was lonely and depressed, however, he still turned to homosexual pornography, and a couple of times he was unfaithful to his wife because of brief homosexual encounters. Martin was full of guilt and frustration. He was tempted to give up on his Christian faith because he was such a failure.

In spiritual counseling, it was meditation on the Sorrowful and Glorious Mysteries that helped Martin the most. He came to understand that his stumbling attempts to follow Christ were actually what it was all about. He started to see his Christian life as a constant battle rather than an instant victory. Visualizing the Resurrection helped Martin keep going. He said, "If Jesus got up from the dead, I'd better keep getting up when I fall." As time went by, this truth helped Martin enormously, and through counseling and the grace of confession he has been able to move toward the full healing of his distorted sexuality.

Pray for Healing

Can you visualize Jesus actually rising from the dead? Can you see the life coming back into his body and the power and the glory of his resurrected body? His disciples didn't recognize him at first — this is because his fully human and glorified body was of a different order than his old body, so torn and broken by sin. Can you glimpse the magnificent pure power in Christ's resurrected body? This is the complete and full humanity that he wants to share with us.

Do you suffer from some weakness or failure that you can't seem to get the victory over? Do you fall into physical sin of which you are ashamed and embarrassed? You mean well, and you want to live in the full power and glory of Christ's resurrection, but do you drift back into old habits, old negative ways of seeing yourself and others, old negative emotions and attitudes?

What is important is not how often you fall, but how often you get up. Can you see how the power of Jesus to rise from the dead is a constant source of power that is always available to you? Visualize that power flowing into your life. You can only overcome sin by God's powerful grace, and the grace released by the Resurrection is overwhelming. Imagine that power and grace filling your life and giving you the strength to keep on fighting your own battles against the world, the flesh, and the devil.

Thank God for This Gift

Father in heaven, deliver us from evil, and let us not be overcome by temptation. By the power of your Son, Jesus Christ, who rose from the dead, help me to keep on fighting the powers of evil in my life. Grant me the power to never give up, until at last I am brought to the final victory of Christ's resurrection. Amen.

ASCENSION
Watching and Waiting for Total Fulfillment

Then he led them out as far as Bethany, and lifting up his hands he blessed them. While he blessed them, he parted from them, and was carried up into heaven.

LUKE 24:50-51

After his resurrection, Jesus' mission was finished and he had to return to his Father in heaven. He gathered his disciples together, teaching them and showing them more of the Father's plan. After giving them final instructions to go into all the world to preach the gospel, he was received into heavenly glory.

Sometimes it is difficult to accept such supernatural events, but C. S. Lewis points out how practical the Ascension was. After all, Jesus had to go somewhere. He would never die again, and his resurrection body couldn't remain on earth forever. His return to the Father was the logical and sensible thing to happen. It was the final chapter of the story. And after the apostles had witnessed his disappearance, two angels appeared, promising them that Jesus would return, and that the apostles were to return and wait for the promised gift of the Holy Spirit.

Think It Through

It must have been amazing to witness the resurrection and ascension of Jesus Christ. Those days between his rising from the dead and his return to the Father in heaven must have been precious and intimate. He was suddenly so real, and his victory over death was overwhelming in its beauty, power, and glory. The truths he was teaching his disciples must have been beautiful and marvelous and profound. The glory moments in our spiritual life are precious — and it's tempting to make them last, or to artificially create such spiritual high points, or to spend time and effort trying hard to find those high points again.

Unfortunately, the Christian life is not quite like that. Jesus goes away and leaves us here to get on with a job. We drift along in the spiritual life, often losing our way, getting discouraged, and wondering what God is up to. If we're not careful, we can start a search for some wonderful kind of life that is only a fantasy. We search for happiness in all sorts of artificial ways that only bring confusion, disappointment, loneliness, and finally loss of faith.

Sometimes we use our faith to create a fantasy spiritual world, or we use our faith to run from reality, creating a false fortress of safety and spiritual coziness. When we do this, disaster is waiting. Twisting religion in this way brings heartache, makes us self-righteous, and defeats the whole purpose of the Christian life.

As we meditate on the glorious ascension of Christ, we must also meditate on how practical Christ's commands are. He takes time to train and teach us, but that is because we have a job to do. He allows us to share in the glories of his victory and his return to heaven, but that is only to charge our batteries and inspire us to continue his work on earth. As we see him ascend into heaven, we must also hear his command to go into all the world to preach and live the glorious gospel he came to give us and the glorious redemption he won for the world.

Healing Example

Anselm was a monk. When he left college, he knew what he wanted to do, and he entered the monastery full of hope for the future. The monastery seemed to be everything he wanted. He pursued a life of prayer. He had time on his own. The liturgy was beautiful. Anselm was musically gifted and soon became the choirmaster, and then editor of the monastery's prestigious theological journal. Whenever I saw Anselm, his habit was spotless and neatly pressed. He was young, good looking, intelligent, and charming. Unfortunately, Anselm was unconsciously using the perfectly glorious religious life of the monastery to escape from a grim reality.

Anselm was a pedophile. In his times alone, he collected and circulated sexual images of children. He was caught, and he exchanged his monastic cell for a prison cell. It seemed to me that perhaps he had focused too much on the glory of the religious life and not enough on the reality of who he was and the serious spiritual work he had to do. This deception at the heart of his existence eventually destroyed his religious life.

The last I heard, Anselm was living an ordinary life and working as a traveling salesman to pay the bills. Maybe the down-to-earth reality of that life will bring the healing he really needs.

Pray for Healing

Can you see Jesus during the forty days leading up to the Ascension walking with his disciples and teaching them about God's plan for the world? At the end of this time, they asked: "Is this the time for God's kingdom to be established?" (see Acts 1:6). They wanted Jesus to remain on earth as king, but that would have been the easy way. Instead, Jesus asked them to spread the word and build the kingdom. How were they feeling as he was taken from them? On the one hand, they must have been struck with wonder by the glorious sight. On the other hand, there must have been a sinking feeling at the enormity of the task ahead.

It is great to dream of a positive future and then take action to make it come true. But dreams alone can be a dead end. Are you inclined to dream about the great and wonderful things that might be? Do you indulge too much in a fantasy life? The fantasies might be sexual or linked with fame and fortune. These are unreal, and the pursuit of them will only lead to a life that is a lie. At the heart of the glorious Ascension is glorious reality. The light of the glorious Ascension is given so that we might see more clearly. Jesus is taken so that we can get on with the task at hand — and that task is always practical, hard working, and extraordinarily real.

Be with Jesus during those forty days. Listen to his voice. Is he giving you a special job to do? Have you wasted time fantasizing about some unreal future? Let the supernatural common sense of the resurrected Jesus heal you of that tendency. Ask him to grant you a clear vision and to experience a clear calling.

Have you been wounded by someone in your life who has pulled you into their fantasy life? You may have fallen for a lie and been drawn into an occult or sexual subculture. You may have fallen under the spell of a person who was feeding you lies for his or her own pleasure. You may be under the spell of the fantasy of too much television, internet pornography, or some other obsession. Allow the practical, realistic glory of the Ascension to penetrate your heart and heal you. Let Jesus teach you the Truth, show you the Way, and bring you into Life.

Thank God for This Gift

Father God, I want the beauty and glory of reality. Help me to turn away from artificial dreams, fantasies, and the pursuit of lies. Teach me the Truth, show me the Way, and bring me into the everlasting Life of Jesus Christ, your Son, my Lord. Amen.

PENTECOST
Receiving the Fullness of the Holy Spirit

And suddenly a sound came from heaven like the rush of a mighty wind, and it filled all the house where they were sitting. And there appeared to them tongues as of fire, distributed and resting on each one of them. And they were all filled with the Holy Spirit and began to speak in other tongues, as the Spirit gave them utterance.

ACTS 2:2-4

They were waiting. The angels had told them to go back to Jerusalem and prepare for the task ahead, and all they could do was watch and wait for the gift that had been promised. These eleven timid men waited, with the mother of Jesus in their midst. Then the supernatural gift of the Holy Spirit was poured out. There was a rushing wind, and flames of fire hovered over each of them. The power that filled them was so amazing that they staggered and keeled over. They were accused of being drunk. Suddenly, their natural gifts were amplified by God's power. They became supercharged preachers, teachers, ministers, healers, and exorcists. Filled with God's power, they went out and changed the world.

Think It Through

Isn't that what we really want to do? We want to be used by God. We want our natural gifts to be amplified and used to their fullness. We want to be successful in the deepest sense. We want to change ourselves, change our communities, and change our world for the better. Wouldn't it be wonderful if our own lives could be so filled with the Holy Spirit that Jesus lives in us like a burning fire? Wouldn't it be fantastic if this fire could burn up all the impurities in our lives and supercharge our small lives with divine purity and power?

We long for this total transformation, but we are also frightened of it. Are we really ready to yield ourselves totally? Do we really want the total infilling of the Holy Spirit? Are we really prepared to have every last bit of selfishness, pride, envy, and lust burnt out of our lives? Most of us hold out. We resist and run from the overwhelming glory of the Holy Spirit. We do this in various ways. Some of us run from the hound of heaven into worldly pursuits, shallow enterprises, and selfish ambitions. Others get busy for God, working hard to get things right, to serve others with our energies and to worship God in the "right" way. We prefer our own good works and correct worship to the totally transforming power of the Holy Spirit.

As we meditate on the descent of the Holy Spirit, we should think of all the things we do that remain untouched by the Holy Spirit's power. Our sins and selfishness are obviously parts of our lives that remain untouched by the Holy Spirit. But what about all the good works, the prayers, and worship that we have done simply in our own power, and in our sincere desire to "get it right"? These works are worth nothing if they are not filled with the grace and power of the Holy Spirit. Many of our illnesses are stress related, or linked with sin in our lives. How many illnesses, anxieties, cares, and diseases do we carry because we will not allow the healing power of the Holy Spirit to really transform our lives through and through?

Healing Example

As a young Anglican priest, I thought I had all the answers. I had been through seminary and started my ministry with great enthusiasm. People said I was a good preacher. The youth work in the parish was thriving, and people were full of admiration and praise for my work. I said my prayers, visited the people, and worked hard. Unfortunately, it was all my own effort. I believed the right doctrines in my head. I did the right deeds with my body, but my heart was empty and cold.

Finally, the Lord broke me down. I began to come apart emotionally. At that time, I met a Catholic priest who was active in the renewal movement. He counseled me, listened to me, and loved me as a person. Through him my cold heart began to thaw. After a time of waiting and watching and asking, I began to know the power of the Holy Spirit. The infilling I experienced was like an earthquake in my life. Everything was seen in a different light. A new energy surged through me. Eventually, God started to put me back together again.

That work isn't finished, but the difference is that now I know I can do nothing without that infilling of the Holy Spirit. Now that I'm a Catholic I am reminded of this every time I see an image of the Sacred Heart of Jesus. There I see the burning heart of love that only the Holy Spirit can give, and which I pray will transform my own life.

Pray for Healing

Can you put yourself in that room watching and waiting with the apostles and the Blessed Virgin? The waiting time was a time of reflection, inner searching, and anticipation. Your meditation on this glorious mystery is a time for you to watch and wait for a new infilling of the Holy Spirit. The Scriptures say that if you ask for this infilling, it will be given to you. Take time now to examine everything in your life that has yet to be transformed by the fire of God's love.

Can you open those closed doors to Christ? Can you place all things on the altar of God's love and wait for the fire from heaven that will consume all that is waste, and purify all that is gold? Have the courage to ask for this gift.

Do you get involved in lots of good activities that do not really have anything to do with your faith? Are you concerned first about money, prestige, and worldly success and influence? Do you rush about doing good for God only in your own power? Are you trying to be a "good Catholic" with lots of prayer, worship, and good deeds? Are you anxious about whether other people believe the right doctrines or worship God in the "correct" way? Why not ask first if your life has ever really been transformed by the power of the Holy Spirit? If you have not been touched by the power of the Holy Spirit, then your works are only fueled by your own energy, and not by the Divine Energy of the Holy Spirit.

God's goal for us is to be like him. This can only happen as we yield every last part of our lives to him. We can only be purified like gold in the fire if we allow the Holy Spirit to melt us, mold us, refine us, and remake us in the image of Christ. The Blessed Virgin is in the midst of the apostles at the descent of the Holy Spirit because she has a special link with the Holy Spirit by virtue of her direct link with Jesus Christ.

In your meditation, focus on her. Ask her to pray for your infilling of the Holy Spirit — and be prepared for a healing power that will penetrate to the very depths of your body, mind, and spirit.

Thank God for This Gift

Heavenly Father, I am watching and waiting for the healing gift of the Holy Spirit. Still my heart and mind, reveal what needs to be brought into your healing presence, and then by the intercession of Mary my Mother, fill my life totally and utterly with the fire of your love. This I pray through Christ your Son, my Lord. Amen.

ASSUMPTION
Dying Peacefully

But God, who is rich in mercy, out of the great love with which he loved us, even when we were dead through our trespasses, made us alive together with Christ (by grace you have been saved), and raised us up with him, and made us sit with him in the heavenly places in Christ Jesus, that in the coming ages he might show the immeasurable riches of his grace in kindness toward us in Christ Jesus.

EPHESIANS 2:4-7

In quiet humility, Mary passed the rest of her earthly life in the background. Tradition tells us that she lived with the apostle John until the time came for her to leave her earthly life. We aren't sure how it happened, or who was there at the time, but the simplest version of the story is that Mary was surrounded by the apostles when she died, or "fell asleep." Afterward, her body was not in the tomb, and the Church realized that, just as she shared in her Son's life and death in an intimate way, she must also have shared in his resurrection in a unique way. Because she shared in his physical life, Mary must have shared in his eternal life. Because she shared in his sorrows, she also shared in his ultimate and total victory.

Think It Through

Jesus' death was a cruel and hideous public torture. Mary's passing was quiet, peaceful, and private. Jesus took on the sin of the world and the fury of Satan. Mary passed away in quiet confidence in her Savior. Jesus died feeling forsaken by God.

Mary passed into the arms of her Son in peaceful sleep. This is the ideal death for a Christian — to pass away with all problems resolved, at peace with God, and with a confident hope in eternal life through the death of Christ.

Death, however, even for those who believe in Christ, is not always the peaceful blessing that it must have been for Mary. People are killed violently, painfully, or without having a chance to repent. Others linger for years through painful illness, disability, or a wasting disease. Because of this, it is easy to become fearful about death. It is easy to become bitter if we have witnessed a loved one go through a terrible death. Despite the bitterness of physical death, the assumption of Mary shows us how spiritual healing can still take place within the mystery of physical death.

By meditating on the "falling asleep" of the Blessed Virgin, we can glimpse what sort of death we might wish for and ask God to bless us with a passing that is full of quiet confidence in his redeeming work. We can also bring into God's healing presence all our fears of death, and the bitterness we may feel over some grief from a past death for which we still feel pain. The peaceful death of the Blessed Virgin was a sharing in the victory over death her Son won for mankind. As we meditate on the Assumption, we can pray for healing in the whole area of facing death, bereavement, and fear of death.

Healing Example

My mother lost her father at Christmastime when she was just sixteen. My grandfather was walking across an icy bridge with his two young sons when a coal-truck driver lost control. The laden truck slid across the ice and smashed into him as he jumped to push his boys out of the path. Well-meaning witnesses to the accident folded his broken body into the back of a car to take him to the hospital, but as they did this his broken ribs punctured his inner organs. Grief and shock crashed into my mother's life.

The next years were hard for her family, and the sudden and tragic death of her father seemed absurd and cruel in her eyes. However, something beautiful also had happened, which helped her to face the tragic loss. When Grandfather was in the hospital dying, my mother tells the story of how he suddenly drifted back into consciousness. Grandmother was at his bedside. His eyes opened and he sat up. He looked up to the corner of the room and said, "Can't you see them? Can't you see them? They're so beautiful!" — then he fell back and was gone.

This wonderful Christian death became a huge comfort to my mother, and it has helped our whole family face the reality of death and dying. It really is true that those who die *fall asleep in the Lord* (see 1 Thess 4:13), and meditating on the final events of Mary's life remind us that, like her, we, too, have the hope of sharing in the resurrection of her Son, Jesus Christ.

Pray for Healing

Can you envision the peaceful and glorious death the Blessed Virgin must have experienced? She simply went to sleep and woke up in heaven. The apostles and family members who were there must have been inspired by her holy death.

Can you see the love she shared with them, radiant in their faces? Can you see their tears of grief mixed with joy at the realization that one day they, too, could face death with confident hope in Christ's resurrection? Can you feel the emotions of that moment when they realized that her body was gone and that God had performed a miracle to take her, body and soul, into heaven? If they had held any lingering doubts, the promise of the Resurrection was now as real for them as it had ever been. One day, in due time, they, too, would share in the bodily resurrection — not in the unique way Mary did, but in their own way, as they shared in the life of Christ.

What has your experience of death been like? Are there any unresolved deaths in your family? Is there a miscarriage, a stillbirth, or an aborted child who has never been properly mourned? Was there a violent, painful, or distressing death that was never acknowledged? Do you suffer the pain of prolonged bereavement? Do you fear death? Are you over-protective or anxious about death — or like many people, do you deny death and pretend it is never going to happen?

Bring your attitudes, your grief and bereavement, and your fears and pains into this meditation. Witness the beautiful and glorious death of the Virgin and see that you, too, can share in the glory of Christ's resurrection. Yield your cares and fears to her in her simple and quiet passing. If there is an unresolved death, ask your priest to offer a Mass for the departed person. This will also help your own healing in the face of death.

Thank God for This Gift

Heavenly Father, thank you for the victory of Christ Jesus over death. Thank you for the beautiful way he shared that victory by taking his mother to heaven, body and soul, after her earthly life was over. Grant me healing from all my fears, gather my loved ones into your eternal life, and give me a confident hope and peaceful assurance of Christ's forgiving love in the face of my own death. Amen.

CORONATION
Being All We Were Created to Be

And a great sign appeared in heaven, a woman clothed with the sun, with the moon under her feet, and on her head a crown of twelve stars; she was with child and she cried out in her pangs of birth, in anguish for delivery.

REVELATION 12:1-2

We don't have an eyewitness to the happenings in heaven after Mary's arrival there, but the Book of Revelation gives us the next best thing. The apostle John has visions of heaven and the end of all things. In one of the visions, recorded in the twelfth chapter, John sees a woman "clothed with the sun, with the moon under her feet, and on her head a crown of twelve stars." This woman's son is the Messiah, the ruler over all, and this reveals the woman to be the Mother of the Messiah — Mary. From this vision of heaven, the Church has praised God for the final glory that Jesus shares with his mother — a share in his eternal kingdom as the Queen of Heaven.

Think It Through

As Mary takes her place in heaven, she becomes all that she was created to be. At the Annunciation, the angel said her Son would be the King of Israel, so even then her identity as the Queen Mother was established. Her life and destiny are fulfilled in her Son, and she reflects his glory as the moon reflects the sun. Around her head are the stars that represent the twelve tribes of Israel and the twelve apostles. As such, the stars also stand for the Church and all the saints. As Queen of Heaven, she sits amidst the whole created order in her right and proper place. No longer the simple girl from Nazareth, she takes her seat at the heart of love as the Mother of the Church, the Mother of the baptized, the Mother of all who stand at the cross — and, therefore, our Mother. Her coronation is the final fulfillment of God's work in her life.

So often, here on earth, in our little lives, we lose sight of our final glory. We get confused by life's trials, tempted by sin, and our vision becomes darkened by sin, lies, self-doubt, and the world's deception. We get weighed down by anxieties, fears, and disappointments. Our lives get burdened with illness, grief, lust, and rage. We forget who we are and what our lives are for. We lose the vision of our final destiny and drift along in a muddled mentality of self-pity, low self-esteem, and despair.

By meditating on the coronation of the Blessed Virgin, we are reminded that there is a special eternal glory awaiting each one of us. God made us to be citizens of heaven. There is a place in the circle of the stars waiting for us. In his overall plan, the Creator has a role for us to play, and a home for us to go to. As we meditate on Mary receiving her reward and taking her final place of glory, we should remember that Jesus has gone to prepare a place for us, and that place is far more glorious and abundant than we can ever imagine. The unique place God has for each one of us springs from his total and unconditional love for each of his creations. Mary was created to become the Queen of Heaven, and each one of us was created to become a prince or princess in that kingdom.

Healing Example

Marian came to see me with ME — also known as chronic fatigue syndrome, a mysterious disease that leaves the sufferer totally exhausted. Sometimes there are other mysterious symptoms — sufferers can't bear too much light and have to live in darkened rooms. Sometimes they can't find the energy or confidence to even go out, so they become reclusive and lonely.

As I got to know Marian, I realized that along with the ME she had the worst self-image I had ever come across. On the surface, she was a bubbly, optimistic person, but beneath the mask her life was a maze of self-hatred. She hated her appearance and had developed an eating disorder. She hated herself because she had been sexually promiscuous, only to have one man after another break the relationship. She had a terrible relationship with her mother — who constantly criticized Marian, put her down, and insulted her. Underneath it all, Marian suffered from the basic human problem: she did not experience total, unconditional love. She felt worthless. She had never experienced the basic truth that God not only created her, but that he loved her and had a unique and wonderful place for her in his cosmic plan.

Marian began to pray the Rosary, with a focus on this final glorious mystery. After a long period of counseling and staying on the path to recovery, she experienced the love of God in the midst of the liturgy. She described it to me: "The whole liturgy was wonderful. I felt like I was on the doorstep of heaven. When we said the Hail Mary at the end of the Prayers of the Faithful, something opened up. I got a little glimpse of the glory that is waiting for all of us."

Her eyes were glowing as she said, "I can't explain it. I just knew that all my suffering and all my life had a purpose and that it will one day be revealed, and I want that more than anything!" That was the turning point in Marian's therapy. She started to get better, gave up her job as a financial analyst, and joined a Christian community evangelizing in eastern Europe.

Pray for Healing

Can you try to imagine Mary as the Queen of Heaven, with all the saints surrounding her, each one in his or her perfect and proper place? Can you see the multitudes of the faithful, all in their created place — totally fulfilled, totally enraptured, and totally at one with who they are and who they were created to be? Can you see all of them so full of joy and completion of love as they stand in the glory of God — with hearts and voices full of praise? Take time to meditate on this image. Can you see an empty place in that multitude? That is your place. Jesus said, "I am going to prepare a place for you, so that where I am, there you may be too" (see Jn 14:3).

Beneath all your sufferings and pleasure, beneath all your joys and sorrow, beneath all your doubts and faith, your fear and your hope, and your sin and your repentance lies the simple human fault that all of us feel at the very depth of our existence: the lack of love. Each one of us has been created with a longing for love, and that longing for love can only be fulfilled by the totally unconditional love of God. Sexual love cannot fill it. Love of material things cannot fill it. Pleasure cannot fill it. Success and achievement cannot fill it. Status and prestige cannot fill it. Doing the right thing cannot fill it. Beauty cannot fill it. Knowledge cannot fill it. Only God's love can fill that gap.

Mary's coronation shows us the glory of God's love fulfilled in one of his creatures. As you meditate on this mystery, bring your own empty heart to Jesus Christ. Know that he loves you. Know that God has created you as a unique person. You are known and totally loved by him. He has created a place in glory for you, and your journey to that place begins here, today. Today is the day for you to know that total and unconditional love. Open your heart to that love. Plead with God for the knowledge of that love. Only this love will heal your wounds, forgive your sins, redeem your mistakes, and restore you to that eternal glory for which you were created.

Thank God for This Gift

Heavenly Father, in your plan of love, you created the Virgin Mary for eternal glory in your presence. Grant me the knowledge of that eternal love. I plead with you, through the Sacred Heart of Jesus and the Immaculate Heart of Mary, to grant me a deep awareness of your unconditional love — and as I come to know that love, help me to radiate that love to all I meet. This I pray through Christ my Savior. Amen.

APPENDIX
Prayers of the Rosary

Sign of the Cross

In the name of the Father, and of the Son, and of the Holy Spirit. Amen.

Apostles' Creed

I believe in God, the Father almighty, creator of heaven and earth; and in Jesus Christ, his only Son, our Lord; who was conceived by the Holy Spirit, born of the Virgin Mary, suffered under Pontius Pilate, was crucified, died, and was buried. He descended to the dead; the third day he arose again from the dead. He ascended into heaven and sits at the right hand of God, the Father almighty; from thence he shall come to judge the living and the dead. I believe in the Holy Spirit, the holy catholic Church, the communion of saints, the forgiveness of sins, the resurrection of the body, and life everlasting. Amen.

Our Father

Our Father, who art in heaven, hallowed be thy name. Thy kingdom come. Thy will be done on earth, as it is in heaven. Give us this day our daily bread, and forgive us our trespasses, as we forgive those who trespass against us, and lead us not into temptation, but deliver us from evil. Amen.

Hail Mary

Hail Mary, full of grace. The Lord is with thee. Blessed art thou among women, and blessed is the fruit of thy womb,

Jesus. Holy Mary, Mother of God, pray for us sinners, now and at the hour of our death. Amen.

Glory Be

Glory be to the Father, and to the Son, and to the Holy Spirit. As it was in the beginning, is now, and ever shall be, world without end. Amen.

Fátima Prayer

O my Jesus, forgive us our sins, save us from the fires of hell, lead all souls to heaven, especially those who have most need of your mercy. Amen.

Hail, Holy Queen

Hail, holy Queen, Mother of Mercy, our life, our sweetness, and our hope. To thee do we cry, poor banished children of Eve; to thee do we send up our sighs, mourning, and weeping in this valley of tears. Turn then, most gracious advocate, thine eyes of mercy toward us, and after this, our exile, show unto us the blessed fruit of thy womb, Jesus. O clement, O loving, O sweet Virgin Mary.

V. Pray for us, O Holy Mother of God.
R. That we may be made worthy of the promises of Christ.

Concluding Rosary Prayer

Let us pray: O God, whose only begotten Son, by his life, death, and resurrection, has purchased for us the rewards of eternal life, grant, we beseech thee, that meditating upon these mysteries of the Most Holy Rosary of the Blessed Virgin Mary, we may imitate what they contain and obtain what they promise, through the same Christ our Lord. Amen.

ABOUT THE AUTHOR

DWIGHT LONGENECKER is a former Evangelical. After studying theology at Oxford University, he was ordained as an Anglican priest and served as an assistant priest, a school chaplain, and a country pastor. He and his family were received into the Catholic Church in 1995. Since then, he has authored ten books on Catholic apologetics and Benedictine spirituality. He writes regularly for many magazines and newspapers in Great Britain and the United States.

In 2006, Dwight Longenecker was ordained as a Catholic priest under the pastoral provision for married former Anglican priests. He now serves as chaplain to St. Joseph's Catholic School in Greenville, South Carolina. He also ministers at the parish of St. Mary's, Greenville. Visit his website at www.dwightlongenecker.com.